SOUTH AMERICA

A TRUE BOOK

by

David Petersen

A Division of Grolier Publishing

New York London Hong Kong Sydney
Danbury, Connecticut

A victoria
regia lily pad

Reading Consultant
Linda Cornwell
Learning Resource Consultant
Indiana Department of
Education

Visit Children's Press on the Internet at:
http://publishing.grolier.com

Library of Congress Cataloging-in-Publication Data

Petersen, David, 1946–
    South America / by David Petersen.
        p.   cm. — (A true book)
    Includes bibliographical references and index.
    Summary: Introduces the geography, history, climate, and culture of
South America.
    ISBN 0-516-20769-5 (lib.bdg.)   0-516-26440-0 (pbk.)
    1. South America—Description and travel—Juvenile literature.
[1. South America.] I. Title. II. Series.
F2264.2.P48   1998
968—dc21   98-24338
                                                                   CIP
                                                                   AC

Contents

A Land of Diversity   5

The Mighty Amazon   12

The Awesome Andes   19

The Great Central Plains   25

Watery Wonders   32

The People of South America   35

To Find Out More   44

Important Words   46

Index   47

Meet the Author   48

CENTRAL AMERICA

Caribbean Sea

L. Maracaibo

Caracas

VENEZUELA

GUYANA
SURINAME
FR. GUIANA

NORTH ATLANTIC OCEAN

Panama Canal

Bogotá

LLANOS

Georgetown
Paramaribo
Cayenne

COLOMBIA

Equator

Quito

ECUADOR

Amazon River

PERU

SELVAS

BRAZIL

Lima

ANDES MOUNTAINS

L. Titicaca
La Paz

BOLIVIA

Sucre

Brasília

BRAZILIAN HIGHLANDS

Atacama Desert

Tropic of Capricorn

CHILE

PARAGUAY
Asunción

São Paulo
Iguaçu Falls

Rio de Janiero

GRAN CHACO
ARGENTINA

Mt. Aconcagua

URUGUAY

SOUTH ATLANTIC OCEAN

SOUTH PACIFIC OCEAN

Santiago

Buenos Aires

Montevideo

PAMPAS

SOUTH AMERICA

● Capital city

0   600 Miles

0   900 Kilometers

Falkland I. (Br.)

Drake Passage
Cape Horn

Tierro del Fuego

A Land of Diversity

If Earth's seven continents were lined up according to their size, South America would stand in the middle. It's larger than Australia, Europe, and Antarctica, but smaller than Asia, Africa, and North America. Its shape is roughly triangular—widest at the top, narrowing to a point at the bottom.

"South" America actually lies southeast of North America. South and North America are joined by a narrow strip of land called the Isthmus of Panama. Without that slender land connection, South America would be Earth's largest island. The continent is almost completely surrounded by water. The Caribbean Sea is on the north,

Magellanic penguins on
the beaches of Patagonia

the Atlantic Ocean on the
east, the Pacific Ocean on the
west, and the Drake Passage
lies to the south.

The Drake Passage is a sea-
way that separates South
America from frozen Antarctica,

7

600 miles (970 kilometers) farther south. These southern
regions of South America are
home to such cold-loving creatures as penguins and fur seals.

Yet, strange as it seems,
South America also contains
the world's largest jungle.
Jungles, or tropical rain forests,
are always warm, wet, green,
and near the equator.

Equatorial regions get more
sunlight than anywhere else on
Earth, and they have no winter

Rain forests are always warm and wet.

at all. In addition to heat, the abundant sunlight also promotes plant growth. If you add rain, which is plentiful near the equator, you have

The Amazon River is often called the Mar Dulce, meaning "freshwater sea."

the main ingredients for a tropical rain forest.

In South America, the rain forest is called the Selva. Its lifeline is the Amazon River.

Do You Know About the Equator?

Imagine Earth as a basketball. If you poked a stick into the top of the ball, down through its center, and out the bottom, the stick would represent the globe's axis. The Earth completes one spin daily on its axis.

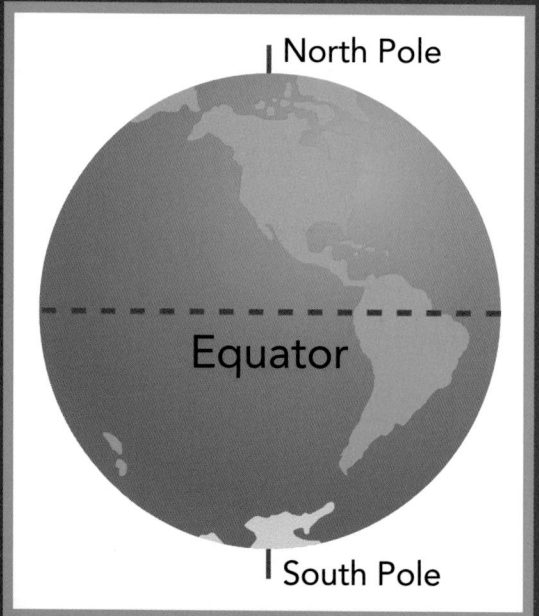

North Pole

Equator

South Pole

The point where the stick enters the top of the ball represents the North Pole. The point where the stick exits from the bottom of the ball is the South Pole. Now if you were to draw a line, like a belt, around the middle of the ball, midway between the two poles—that belt would be the equator.

The Mighty Amazon

Look at a map of South America, and you'll see that the equator crosses the top part of the continent, passing through Ecuador and Brazil. Just below the equator flows the mighty Amazon River.

Stretching for 4,000 miles (6,437 km), the Amazon is the

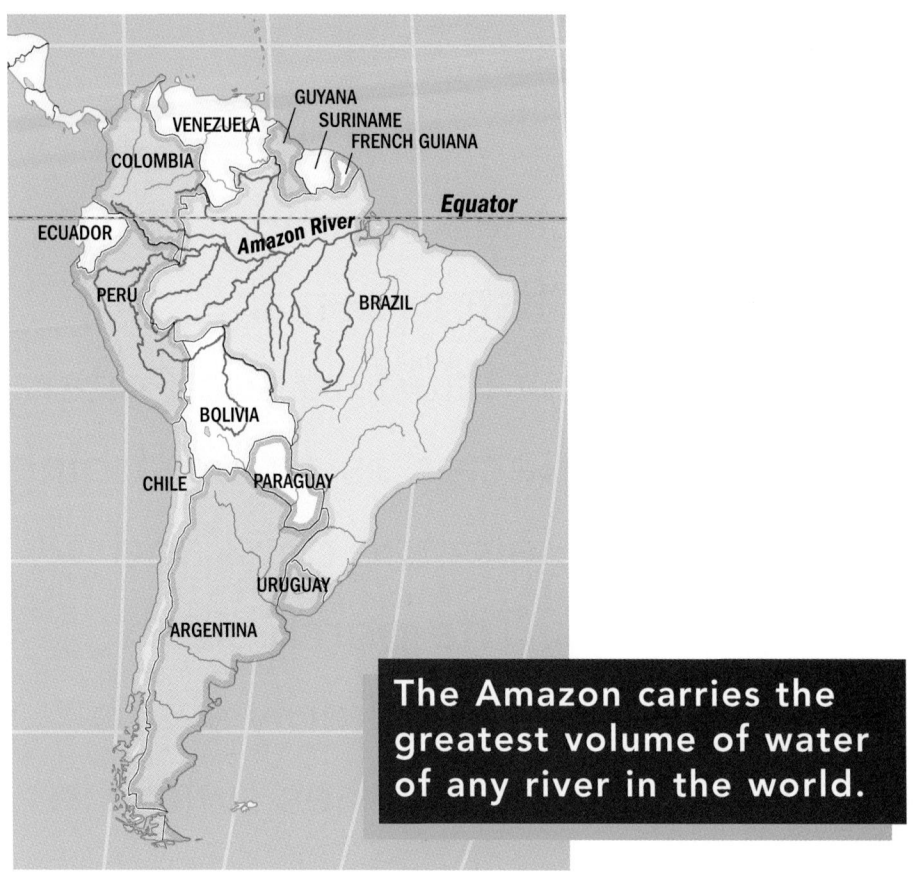

The Amazon carries the greatest volume of water of any river in the world.

world's second-longest river. Only the Nile River in Africa is longer, but the Amazon carries much more water than the Nile.

More than two hundred kinds of fish live in the Amazon, including such interesting species as air-breathing lungfish, electric eels, and piranhas. The perch-sized piranha has wickedly sharp teeth. It sometimes swims in schools and eagerly attacks larger animals.

Many kinds of monkeys swing through the treetops of the Selva. Their noisy neighbors in the forest canopy

The Selva is home to many creatures such as the red-bellied piranha (top left), emperor tamarin monkey (top right), and the red-crowned parrot (left).

include big-billed toucans, colorful parrots and macaws, and other species far too numerous to list.

The most majestic Selva creature is the jaguar, the Americas' largest wildcat. Jaguars have black spots on their golden fur, and big, haunting eyes. They live by hunting meaty jungle residents, such as monkeys and tapirs—(hooved mammals that look a lot like pigs).

Jaguars can weigh up to 400 pounds (180 kilograms).

Another leading member of the Amazon wildlife community is the anaconda, one of the world's largest snakes. These shy reptiles grow 30 feet (9 meters) or more in length.

Save the Rain Forest

The Selva of South America contains more species of plants than any other region on Earth. Here you will find a spectacular array of wild orchids, and more than 2,500 kinds of trees. Many medicines and other important products come from rain forest plants. This great, green tangle of life also produces much of the Earth's oxygen.

Sadly, the rain forest is being logged, strip-mined, burned, ranched, settled, and otherwise destroyed. And with the loss of the rain forest, Earth loses countless plant and animal species forever.

The Awesome Andes

West of the Selva rise the awesome Andes, the world's longest mountain range. The Andes stretch 4,500 miles (7,200 km) along South America's Pacific coast.

The Andes are the second-highest mountains in the world. Only the Himalaya, in

A view of the Andes Mountains in Chile (left) and Mount Aconcagua (below)

Asia, are higher. Many snow-capped Andean peaks rise more than 20,000 feet (6,100 m) above sea level. The tallest of all is Mount Aconcagua in Argentina. Aconcagua soars 22,831 feet (6,959 m) above the nearby Pacific Ocean.

Entirely at home in this lofty habitat are two wild relatives of the camel—the vicuña and the guanaco. Two important domestic animals, the alpaca and the llama, are

A llama

descended from the guana-
co. People use llamas as pack
animals, while alpacas produce the world's finest wool.
 The Andes are also home
to the world's largest flying

The Andean condor is the world's largest flying bird.

bird, the Andean condor. This huge scavenger has a wingspan of about 10 feet (3 m). It glides gracefully for long distances, flapping its wings only once an hour.

The Atacama Desert is one of the driest regions in the world.

Nestled between the Andes Mountains and the Pacific coast is the Atacama Desert—the driest place on earth. From the highest mountains to the driest deserts, South America truly is a land of great natural diversity.

The Great Central Plains

Looking from west to east, South America has three distinct geographical features. Along the western edge of the continent stand the Andes Mountains. The east has the Eastern Highlands of Brazil and Guiana. And between these two mountainous areas sprawl the vast Central Plains.

A view of South America from high above the earth

The Central Plains can be divided into four regions, north to south. The north—Columbia and Venezuela—has an expanse of rolling plains called the Llanos. Water and grass are plentiful here, and cattle ranching is the primary industry.

The Llanos cover more than 100,000 square miles (260,000 sq. km).

South of the Llanos, the lush, wet jungle of the Selva carpets the continent in bright green. The Selva runs along the equator in Peru, Brazil, and Bolivia.

Farther south lie the hardwood scrub forests—the Gran Chaco of Bolivia, Paraguay, and Argentina. This is the hottest part of the continent, where summer temperatures climb as high as 110 degrees Fahrenheit (43 degrees Celsius).

South America's fertile plains are rich ground for farming or for cattle grazing.

The southernmost region of the Central Plains are the vast grasslands of the Argentine Pampa, with rich fertile soil for farming and plenty of grass for sheep and cattle grazing.

Patagonia (above) comes from the Spanish word *patagones* meaning "big feet."

South of the Central Plains and far from the warming equator lies the cool, dry Patagonian plateau. The flightless, ostrich-like rhea is found here. It is the largest bird in the Americas.

Of South America's many off-shore islands, the most interesting are the Galápagos Islands. Here, 600 miles (970 km) off the Pacific coast of Ecuador, live many unusual species of wildlife. You may know about the giant Galápagos turtle, which weighs more than 500 pounds (230 km) and can live for a hundred years.

The giant Galápagos turtle is one of the world's oldest living creatures.

Watery Wonders

South America's largest lake is Maracaibo in Venezuela, covering 5,217 square miles (13,512 sq. km). Perched at 12,507 feet (3,812 m) in the Andes, on the border between Peru and Bolivia, is jewel-like Lake Titicaca—the world's highest navigable lake.

Lake Titicaca (above) is 12,507 feet (3,812 m) above sea level. An aerial view of Angel Falls in Venezuela (right).

With so many rivers and mountains, South America has some of the world's most spectacular waterfalls. The highest is Angel Falls in Venezuela, which plunges more than a half-mile straight down.

The Iguaçu Falls are a favorite tourist attraction in Brazil and Argentina.

Equally impressive is Iguaçu Falls, on the border between Brazil and Argentina. Iguaçu is about as high as a 23-story building, and it forms a thunderous wall of water 2 miles (3.2 km) wide!

The People of South America

The native peoples of South America are Indians whose ancestors arrived at least 11,000 years ago, and possibly much earlier. Until the early 1900s, most South American Indians lived like their ancestors—hunting, fishing, gathering wild plants, and growing

Many Indians in South America still practice the traditions of their ancestors.

small gardens. In the most remote parts of the Selva, a few small tribes still follow this simple way of life.

One of the first groups of South American Indians to

give up the nomadic life of hunting and gathering were the Incas of the Andes Mountains and northern Pacific Coast. Hundreds of years ago, the Incas settled down to become farmers and went on to build great stone cities, create art in gold and gemstones, and rule a power-ful empire. At dozens of archaeological sites, such as Machu Picchu in the Peruvian Andes, magnificent Inca cities

This Inca village in Machu Picchu was abandoned after the Spaniards overthrew the Inca empire in the 1500s.

still stand proudly today. But the once-mighty Inca empire is long dead.

In the 16th century, the Spanish arrived from Europe. In no time, the Inca civilization was destroyed and its fabulous riches were stolen by the Spaniards. The Inca population-shrank from diseases brought by the Europeans, as well as the cruelty of the Spanish invaders.

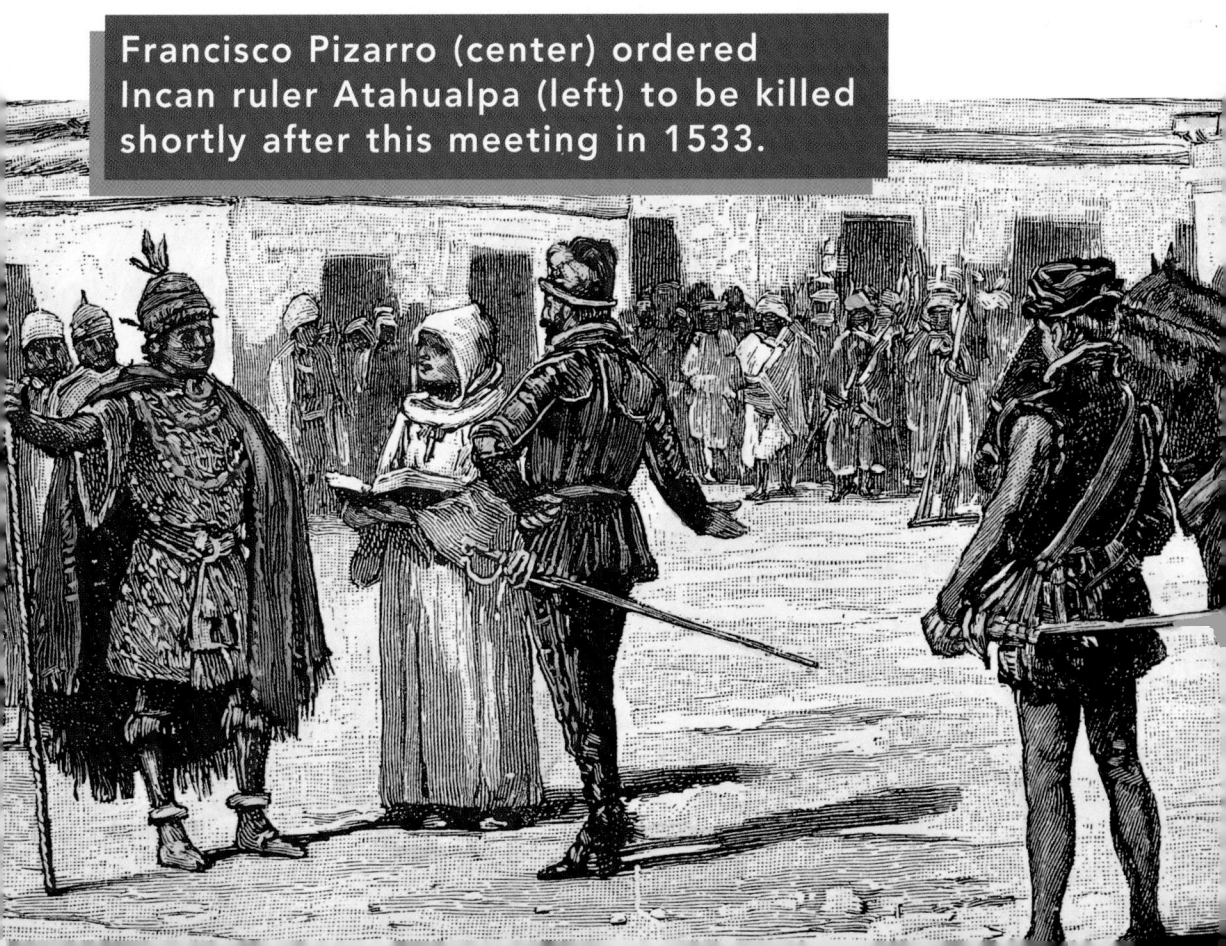

Francisco Pizarro (center) ordered Incan ruler Atahualpa (left) to be killed shortly after this meeting in 1533.

All over South America, other native people suffered similar disasters. Even so, Indians still make up the majority of South America's population today. Many have mixed Indian and European or African ancestry.

In remote areas, traditional native languages are still spo-ken. But in the cities, where 75 percent of South America's 323 million people live, most people speak Spanish. The

A citizen of Chile (left) and a young girl from Peru with her alpaca (right)

exception is Brazil, where Portuguese is spoken.

While modern South America has several large, bustling cities and coastal tourist centers, the continent's real

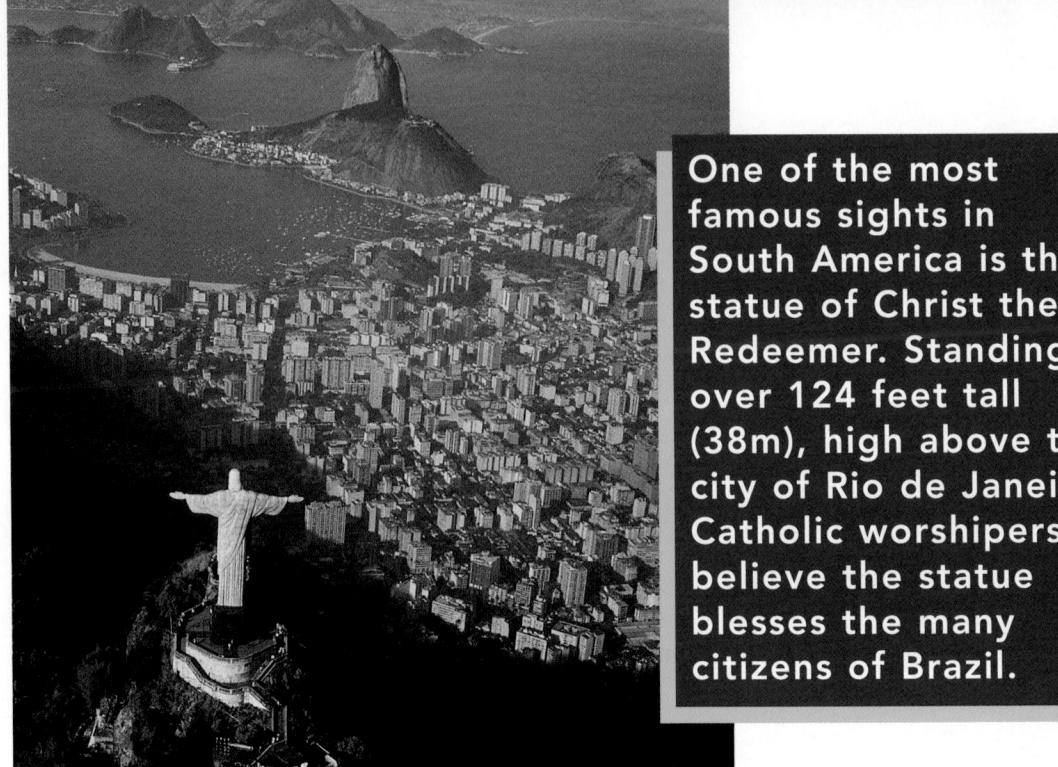

One of the most famous sights in South America is the statue of Christ the Redeemer. Standing over 124 feet tall (38m), high above the city of Rio de Janeiro, Catholic worshipers believe the statue blesses the many citizens of Brazil.

beauty is in the spectacular diversity of its natural wonders—in the jungles, rivers, lakes, waterfalls, and wildlife, and in its native peoples. When you visit South America, these are the sights to see.

South America Fast Facts

Area 6,885,000 square miles (17,833,000 sq. km)

Coastline 20,000 miles (32,000 km)

Highest point Aconcagua Peak, Argentina: 22,831 feet (6,959 m) above sea level

Highest waterfall Angel Falls, Venezuela: 3,212 feet (979 m)

Largest lake Maracaibo, Venezuela: 5,217 square miles (13,512 sq. km)

Longest river Amazon: 4,000 miles (6,437 km)

Lowest point Valdés Peninsula, Argentina: 131 feet (40 m) below sea level

Number of independent nations 12

Population 323 million (1996 estimates)

To Find Out More

Here are some additional resources to help you learn more about the continent of South America:

 **Books**

Planet Earth: World Geography. Oxford University Press, 1993.

Blue, Rose and Corinne Naden. **Andes Mountains.** Raintree Steck-Vaughn, 1994.

Heinrichs, Ann. **Venezuela.** Children's Press, 1997.

Jackson, Alys. **Plains Indians.** Viking Children's Books, 1997.

Myers, Christopher and Lynne. **Galapagos: Islands of Change.** Hyperion Books for Children, 1995.

Reynolds, Jan. **Amazon Basin.** Harcourt Brace, 1993.

Savage, Steven. **Animals of the Rain Forest.** Raintree Steck-Vaughn, 1997.

Steele, Philip. **Incas & Machu Picchu.** Silver Burdett Press, 1993.

Organizations and Online Sites

Explore More Projects for South American Studies
http://www.ospi.wednet.edu:8001/curric/weather/adptcty/projsugg.html

Learn more about the geography, people, and culture of South America while participating in fun projects designed especially for students.

INTELLICast: USA Weather
http://www.intellicast.com/weather/intl/hisasat/

Forecasts and weather information for South America and other continents around the globe.

NOVA/ Ice Mummies of the Inca
http://www.pbs.org/wgbh/nova/peru/

Journey to the high Andes Mountains with a team of archaeologists to unearth frozen mummies from five hundred years ago.

South America Cybertour
http://www.wp.com/virtualvoyager/

This page takes you on a "Cybertour" of South America in seconds! Updated with exciting information, photos, Quicktime movies, and RealAudio sound clips.

Venezuelan Amazon Expedition
http://sunsite.doc.ic.ac.uk/netspedition/amazon.html

Take a journey along the Amazon, including photos, maps, and wildlife.

Important Words

archaeology the study of the physical remains of ancient human cultures

axis the imaginary line around which the earth spins

canopy a protective covering, such as the leafy treetops of a rain forest

geography the study of the earth's surface features, such as continents, oceans, and mountains

habitat the place and natural conditions in which a plant or an animal lives

navigable a body of water wide and deep enough to carry ships

nomad a person who frequently moves, having no permanent home

scavenger an animal or bird that feeds on the remains of dead animals

school a group of fish or other sea creatures swimming together

Index

(**Boldface** page numbers
indicate illustrations.)

Amazon River, 10, **10,**
12–14, **13,** 17
Andes Mountains, 19–24,
20, 25, 32, 36, 37
Angel Falls, 33, **33**
animals, 8, 14–17, **15, 17,**
21–23, **22, 23,** 30, 31, **31**
Antarctica, 5, 7
Argentine Pampa, 29
Atacama Desert, 24, **24**
Atlantic Ocean, 7
Brazil, 12, 25, 28, **34,** 41,
42
Caribbean Sea, 6
Central Plains, 25, 26,
29, 30
Drake Passage, 7
Eastern Highlands, 25
Ecuador, 12, 31
electric eels, 14
equator, 8, 9, 11, 12, 28,
30
Galápagos Islands, 31

Galápagos turtle, 31, **31**
Gran Chaco, 28
Himalayas, 19
Iguaçu Falls, 34, **34**
Incas, 37, 38, 39, **39**
Isthmus of Panama, 6
Lake Titicaca, 32, **33**
Llanos, 27, **27,** 28
lungfish, 14
Machu Picchu, 37, **38**
Maracaibo Lake, 32
Mount Aconagua, **20,** 21
Nile River, 13
North America, 5, 6
Pacific coast, 19, 24, 31,
37
Pacific Ocean, 7, 21
Patagonia, **7,** 30, **30**
piranhas, 14, **15**
rain forests, 8, **9,** 10, 18,
18
Selva, 10, 14, **15,** 16, 18,
18, 19, 28, 36
South American Indians,
35–42, **36**
Spanish, 38–40, **39**

Meet the Author

David Petersen writes about nature and the world. His most recent book is *The Nearby Faraway: A Personal Journey through the Heart of the West* (Johnson Books).

He has written dozens of books for Children's Press, including True Books on national parks and all the continents of the world. David lives in a cabin on a mountain in Colorado. He likes to read, write, walk with his dogs in the woods, camp, hunt, fish, and explore the world.

CATICORN
CRAFTS

CATICORN CRAFTS

25 PURR-FECTLY ENCHANTED PROJECTS

Crystal Allen
Hello Creative Family

Skyhorse Publishing

Artwork on pages 5, 121, and 148, as well as starbursts appearing throughout book, used with permission from Brooke Berry of Brooklyn Berry Designs

Skyhorse Publishing books may be purchased in bulk at special discounts for sales promotion, corporate gifts, fund-raising, or educational purposes. Special editions can also be created to specifications. For details, contact the Special Sales Department, Skyhorse Publishing, 307 West 36th Street, 11th Floor, New York, NY 10018 or info@skyhorsepublishing.com.

Skyhorse® and Skyhorse Publishing® are registered trademarks of Skyhorse Publishing, Inc.®, a Delaware corporation.

Visit our website at www.skyhorsepublishing.com.

10 9 8 7 6 5 4 3 2 1

Library of Congress Cataloging-in-Publication Data is available on file.

Cover design by Daniel Brount
Cover photo credit: Crystal Allen

Print ISBN: 978-1-5107-5100-2
Ebook ISBN: 978-1-5107-5102-6

Printed in China

For my husband for his unwavering support.

For my daughter, Bella, and my son, Adam, for being a constant source of inspiration.

For my mom, from whom I learned to be creative.

For my dad, who always believed I should be a writer.

And for my sister, who was my best friend when I was a unicorn-loving kid and is still my best friend now that I'm a caticorn-loving adult.

Contents

Introduction	1
Safety Information	2
Purr-ty No-Sew Caticorn Pillow	7
Unicorn Kitty Desktop Pencil Holder	13
"Have A Purr-fectly Meowgical Day" Caticorn Card	17
Meowgical Unicorn Kitty Flair Pins	21
Caticorn Flower Pot	25
Cotton Candy Caticorn Bath Bombs	29
Purr-ty Painted Caticorn Rocks	35
Smitten Kitten Ombre Caticorn Picture Frame	39
Sleepy Kitty No-Sew Sleep Mask	43
Caticorn Wrapped Present	47
Groovy Kitty Caticorn Charm Bracelet	51
DIY Rainbow Popsicle Stick Letterboard Sign	55
Curl Up with a Good Book Caticorn Page Corner Bookmarks	59
Sleepy Kitty Caticorn Dream Catcher	65
DIY Caticorn Letterboard Artwork	69
Unicorn Kitty Painted Mason Jar	75
Strike a Purr-ty Pose Caticorn Masquerade Mask	79
Hungry Kitty Caticorn Lunch Bag	83
Meowgical Caticorn Paper Lantern	87
Love the Purr-ty Planet Upcycled Caticorn Planter	91
Caticorns and Confetti Rainbow Popcorn	95
Caticorn Popcorn Boxes	99
No-Sew Caticorn Cup Cozy	103
Better than a Ball of Yarn Rainbow Pom-Pom Pencil Toppers	109
No-Sew Cutie Kitty Caticorn Costume	115
Acknowledgments	121
About the Author	123
Templates	125

INTRODUCTION

Get ready for rainbows, glitter, flowers, and all-things Meowgical (along with a healthy dose of cat puns)!

My name is Crystal Allen, and I am the creator of Hello Creative Family, a website where I inspire families to get creative with quick and easy crafts and recipes (most of which take an hour or less to make). I'm a firm believer that *everyone* has creativity inside them; it's just a matter of finding the thing that sparks their creative spirit.

When I was a tween and teen, I was *obsessed* with unicorns, crafting, and my cat (her name was Battlecat). That's why I'm *so excited* that I was able to create *Caticorn Crafts*!!! (Can you tell with all my exclamation points?!?!?)

The ten-year-old girl inside me is freaking out that I grew up to write a craft book about caticorns. The grownup woman in me is over the rainbow excited that I got to write a craft book filled with sparkles and rainbows and that hopefully will spread a whole lot of happiness.

I kept crafters of all experience levels in mind when writing this book. A few projects I had on my original "caticorn crafts wish list" didn't make the caticorn cut because they proved to be too challenging, and I didn't want to pass that frustration on to others. I'm confident that each project in this book can be created by you the reader. My wish is that you will experience as much joy and happiness when crafting with this book as I did while creating the projects!

Each project has a list of materials, step-by-step instructions, and lots of pictures to help you along the way. At the end of this book, you will find templates for some of the crafts, as well as a few options for caticorn eyes, noses, flowers, and horns that you can trace for the different projects.

Keep your eyes out for my Pro Crafter Tips scattered among the pages of this book. They are filled with little tidbits of knowledge from my last thirty years of crafting!

Are you ready to go somewhere over the rainbow to the magical land of *Caticorn Crafts*? Read on!

P.S. Nothing makes me happier than to see the projects that I've inspired and to hear from my readers! Share your projects on social media using the hashtag #CaticornCrafts and email me at crystal@hellocreativefamily.com.

Safety Information

We hope that caticorn lovers of all ages will have hours of fun creating Meowgical projects from *Caticorn Crafts*. We want you to be safe while you create all of these purr-ty projects!

Keep safe while making caticorn crafts by:

- Always having an adult present to supervise the making of caticorn crafts.
- Checking the safety labels for the tools, materials, and supplies that you are using and following their safety instructions.
- Some of the projects in this book use materials that can be choking hazards that are best not handled by those under the age of three years old. Be mindful of who is crafting next to you!

Look for these safety stickers throughout the book and follow these best practices with adult supervision:

 *Spray Paint:* Use in a well-ventilated area. Keep spray paint cans away from heat, heat sources, and fire. Do not puncture, incinerate, or burn spray paint cans. Keep spray paint on your project (not you!). Make sure not to spray-paint in your eyes or on your face. Use safety glasses, ventilation masks, and gloves. If spray paint gets on skin, wash well with soap and water.

 *Glue Gun:* Protect the surface you are crafting on by using a drip mat. Keep long hair pulled back and consider using heat-resistant gloves to avoid burning fingers. Do not touch the nozzle of a hot glue gun. Never leave a glue gun unattended. If you burn yourself with a glue gun, do not attempt to remove the hot glue from your skin. Plunge skin into cool water until burning sensation subsides and then carefully remove the cooled glue. If you get hot glue in your eyes, rinse thoroughly with cold water and seek medical attention immediately.

 **Scissors and Craft Knives:** Never run with, engage in horseplay with, or point and wave around scissors or craft knives. Always hold with blade facing down when moving from one location to another. Cut away from your body. Focus on the task at hand when using scissors or craft knives. Stop using your tool if you want to look up. Use in a well-lit area. Only use scissors and craft knives for their intended cutting purposes. Store craft knives with blade retracted or with a safety cover on it. Store scissors blade-side down.

 Shrinky Dinks in Oven: Use oven-safe gloves for taking sheet pan in and out of oven. Allow shrink plastic to cool before touching. Use a hot pad or wire rack to place hot sheet pans on to protect countertops.

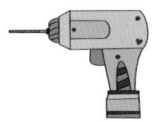 **Drill:** Always tie back long hair and avoid wearing long jewelry or baggy clothing when operating a drill. Wear safety glasses to prevent plastic shavings from going into your eyes.

PROJECTS

Purr-ty No-Sew Caticorn Pillow

When I found out I was going to be writing a caticorn craft book, this was one of the very first projects I imagined. It was so much fun to see come to life, and it turned out even prettier than I had dreamed. The day I finished the project, three preteen girls and one six-year-old boy were in my house. I showed them the pillow, and all four kids took turns passing it around, cuddling it, and saying how much they loved it (there may have been a few squeals from the girls when they first saw it, too!). Their enthusiasm for this project was the confirmation I needed to know that the pillow was just as cute as I thought it was. From the sweet little eyelashes, to the heart-shaped nose, to the pretty watercolor fringe "fur," this pillow is the purr-fect accessory for cuddling up with!

Materials:

- 🐾 20-inch by 36-inch piece of white fleece
- 🐾 Ruler
- 🐾 Painter's tape or masking tape
- 🐾 Scissors
- 🐾 Fabric markers
- 🐾 Felt in white, pink, black, yellow, and whatever colors you want for the horn
- 🐾 Fabric glue
- 🐾 16-inch pillow form

Instructions:

Step 1: Fold your fleece in half and lay it in front of you with the folded edge facing toward you. Use your ruler and tape to create a 2-inch border up the right- and left-hand side and across the top of your fleece.

Step 2: Using the tape as a guide, make cuts every 1 inch through both layers of fleece. Cut through the left- and right-hand side of the fleece as well as the top, but leave the bottom folded edge uncut. Cut out the two top square corners.

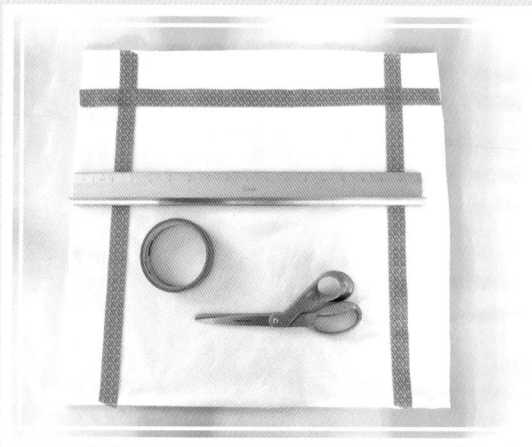
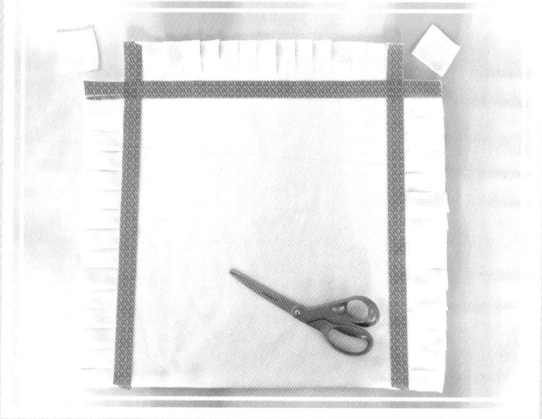

Step 3: Use your fabric markers to color the fringe. Make sure you get both the front and the back of each piece of fringe.

Step 4: While your fringe is drying, cut the pieces for your caticorn's face and horn out of felt using the templates in the back of this book. Glue them to the front of the fleece pillowcase and set aside to dry.

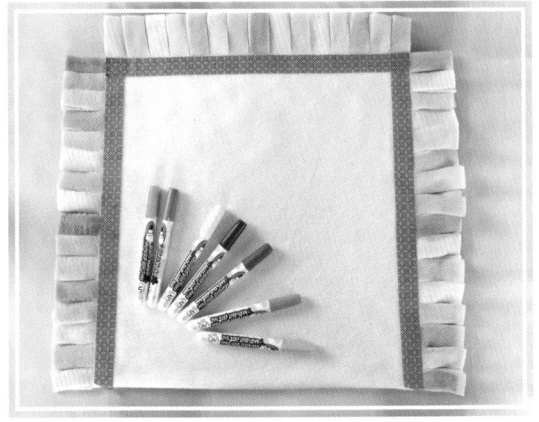

🐾 **Pro Crafter Tip** 🐾
Use a second piece of fleece to blot each piece of fringe to give the "caticorn mane" a light watercolor look.

Step 5: Lay your pillow between the front and the back pieces of fleece. Close your pillowcase by lining up and knotting together your fringe pieces, taking one piece of fringe from the top layer and knotting it to the lined-up piece of fringe from the bottom layer. Work all the way around the pillow, knotting each piece of fringe.

Give yourself a pat on the back and give your new caticorn pillow an extra big cuddle! Isn't it awesome to create handmade things?

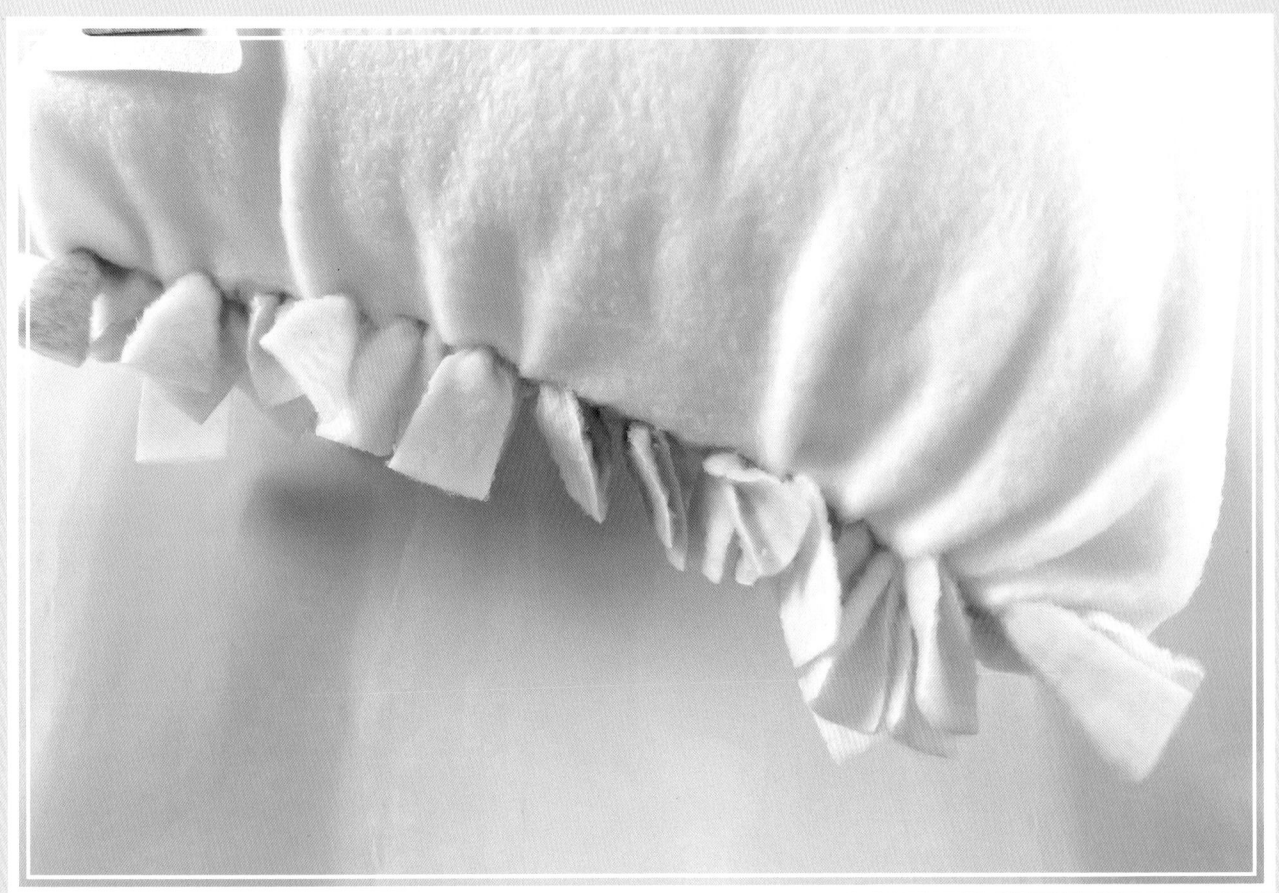

Step 5

Unicorn Kitty Desktop Pencil Holder

Make your desk as "purr-ty" as can be with this adorable unicorn kitty desktop pencil holder! I love reusing items from the recycling bin for my craft projects (check out the Love The Purr-ty Planet Upcycled Caticorn Planter on page 91 for another awesome upcycled project). This pencil holder uses a tin can for the base. I'm giving you the basics for this project, but I encourage you to make it 100 percent your own! Don't feel like cutting out pieces for the face? Draw them on with a marker! Want your unicorn kitty to be sleeping? Cut out a pair of sleepy eyes! Have fun playing with embellishments for your pencil holder! Make a tail out of rainbow-colored yarn, give your unicorn kitty a sparkly nose, or line the inside of the pencil holder with some pretty felt! The possibilities are endless!

Materials:

- Tin can
- Pencil
- Ruler
- Card stock or construction paper
- Scissors
- Glue Dots
- Glue or glue gun
- Optional: Items to embellish your pencil holder with, like paper flowers, sequins, or yarn.

Instructions:

Step 1: Measure your tin can. Use a pencil and ruler to mark the size of the tin can on a piece of card stock or construction paper. Cut out using scissors.

Step 2: Use Glue Dots and glue to attach the paper to your tin can. I like the combination of the Glue Dots and glue because the Glue Dots give you instant stick, where the glue gives you longer-lasting stick once it dries.

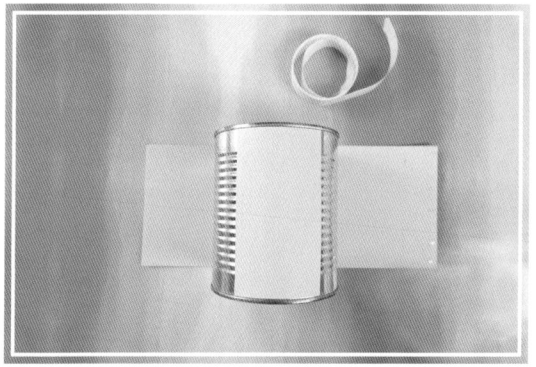

🐾 **Pro Crafter Tip** 🐾
If your paper isn't quite big enough to wrap all the way around your can, cut a second piece to close the gap on the back of the can.

Step 3: Cut ears, horn, eyes, nose, whiskers, mouth, and any other caticorn pieces that you would like out of card stock or construction paper.

Step 4: Glue ears, horn, eyes, nose, whiskers, mouth, and any other caticorn pieces that you have cut out onto your pencil holder. Allow to dry.

Optional step: Embellish with other pretty things! I added some paper flowers and a strip of sequins to my pencil holder to give it a bit more dazzle!

Fill with pencils (like our Better than a Ball of Yarn Rainbow Pom-Pom Pencil Toppers on page 109) and create a magical little workspace!

"Have a Purr-fectly Meowgical Day" Caticorn Card

One of my favorite things in the world is to surprise people with little handmade items. Giving someone something handmade for their birthday is great, but there is nothing better than brightening someone's day when they least expect it. These sweet little caticorn notecards are the purr-fect way to do just that! Slip one in a lunch bag, under a door, on a pillow, or into a locker to surprise a friend or loved one.

Materials:

- White card stock
- Glitter card stock (We used gold for the horn; pink for the cheeks, nose, and inner ears; black for the eyes; and blue for the wings)
- Scissors
- A pen
- Glue (Whatever you like for gluing paper is great! Liquid glue, a glue stick, or Glue Dots all work well)

Instructions:

Step 1: Use our templates in the back of the book to trace each of the Caticorn Card pieces, and then cut them out using scissors. Fold the card piece in half and write a message inside.

Step 2: Glue each of the pieces to your card. Glue the horn, whites of the ears, and wings to the back of the card. Glue the eyes, inner parts of the ear, cheeks, and nose to the front of the card. Make sure to wipe away any excess glue that may have seeped out from beneath the pieces, and then put your card under a heavy book to dry. Surprise someone you care about with this pretty card and brighten their day!

Pro Crafter Tip
Make a whole batch of cards at once and put them away someplace safe so you have a purr-ty card whenever you need one!

Step 2

Meowgical Unicorn Kitty Flair Pins

When I was a kid, three of my favorite things were cats (my kitty's name was Battlecat), unicorns (I had a huge collection of glass unicorn figurines), and crafts! I guess some things never change! I was a kid during the eighties, and one of my very favorite craft projects was Shrinky Dinks! I loved creating bright, colorful creations on these fun pieces of plastic, laying them on a cookie sheet, having my mom pop them in the oven, and watching them shrink down to tiny, brightly colored charms through the window of the oven. For this craft, we're making something else that was popular in the eighties that has made a comeback: flair pins! If you like this craft, make sure you also check out the Groovy Kitty Caticorn Charm Bracelet on page 51 of this book!

Materials:

- Shrinky Dinks Sheets (I love the frosted kind for this project so that you can't see the pin back through your finished pin)
- Markers or colored pencils
- Scissors
- A cookie sheet lined with foil or parchment paper
- Oven or toaster oven
- Pin backs
- E6000 glue or other jewelry glue

Instructions:

Step 1: Draw your unicorn kitty design on your Shrinky Dink sheet and color in. You can use my unicorn kitty drawing at the back of this book as a template.

Step 2: Cut your shapes out of the Shrinky Dink sheet and lay them on a sheet pan lined with either parchment paper or aluminum foil. Follow the instructions on the Shrinky Dink packaging for shrinking your design. (Make sure you have adult supervision for this part.)

Step 3: Put a small dot of E6000 glue on the round part of each pin back and press firmly onto the back of your Shrinky Dink designs. Leave to dry overnight.

Pin your Meowgical Shrinky Dink Unicorn Kitty Flair Pins to your favorite shirt or jacket and get ready to rock that enchanted eighties look!

🐾 Pro Crafter Tip 🐾
Lay your Shrinky Dinks under something heavy like a cutting board as soon as you remove them from the oven. This helps flatten any edges that might be slightly curled.

Step 3

Caticorn Flowerpot

Quick and easy crafts are my favorite kind! I love being able to sit down in my craft room for thirty minutes or less and to be able to walk out having accomplished something! This project is not only adorable, but it's also simple and can be made in about ten minutes! Bonus: it's also really inexpensive! This project would be super fun for a craft night or as a caticorn birthday party make-and-take! Make a whole litter of caticorn flowerpots, plant different colors of flowers in them, and have a rainbow of caticorns lined up on your front porch.

Materials:

- Paint pens or acrylic paint and paintbrushes
- Terra-cotta flowerpot (mine came painted white. If you can't find them pre-painted, give it a coat of your favorite color of paint.)
- Scissors
- Felt
- Glue
- Glitter

Instructions:

Step 1: Use your paint pens (or acrylic paint and paintbrushes) to paint an adorable caticorn face on your flower pot.

Step 2: Cut a caticorn horn out of felt.

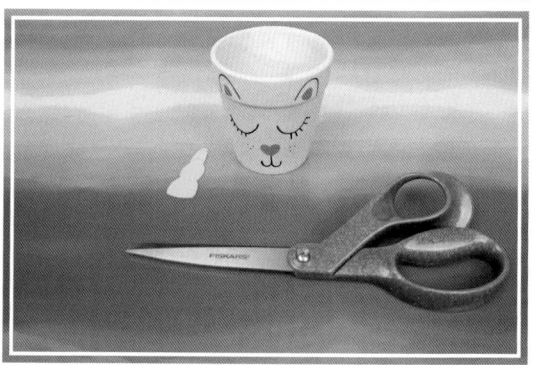

Step 3: Put a thin coat of glue on your felt and then sprinkle it with glitter. Leave it to dry and then tap off excess sparkles.

Step 4: Glue your caticorn horn to your terracotta flower pot.

Fill your flower pot with pretty flowers! Set on your desk, as a centerpiece on a table, or under cover on your front porch or back deck (make sure you don't leave these out in the rain; caticorns hate to get wet!). Pair your Caticorn Flower Pot with the Love the Purr-ty Planet Upcycled Caticorn Planter from page 91 of this book for a pretty caticorn garden!

🐾 **Pro Crafter Tip** 🐾

If you don't have a green thumb, there's no need to fret! I love using faux succulents and silk flowers to decorate my indoor space to avoid needing to water!

Cotton Candy Caticorn Bath Bombs

Bath bombs are one of my favorite things to make when I want to give a handmade gift. Each time I whip up a batch, I feel so amazed that I'm making them with my own two hands instead of buying them from a store for $5 each. I keep bath bomb supplies on hand at all times so that I can whip up a batch at a moment's notice. These bath bombs have a cute little caticorn face and smell like cotton candy—because that's what caticorns smell like! I've given you two options for shapes. The first option is made using meatball tongs, which takes a bit of practice to get right. The second option uses a silicone soap mold. Press your bath bomb mixture into the mold, leave it to dry overnight, and pop them out for an easy-peasy bath bomb shape alternative!

Materials:

- 1 cup baking soda
- ½ cup Epsom salt
- ½ cup citric acid
- ½ cup cornstarch
- A few drops of cotton candy fragrance oil (or your essential oil or fragrance oil of choice)
- 4–6 tablespoons melted coconut oil
- Meatball tongs, bath bomb molds, or silicone soap mold
- Mica powder in your desired colors
- Isopropyl alcohol
- Small paintbrush

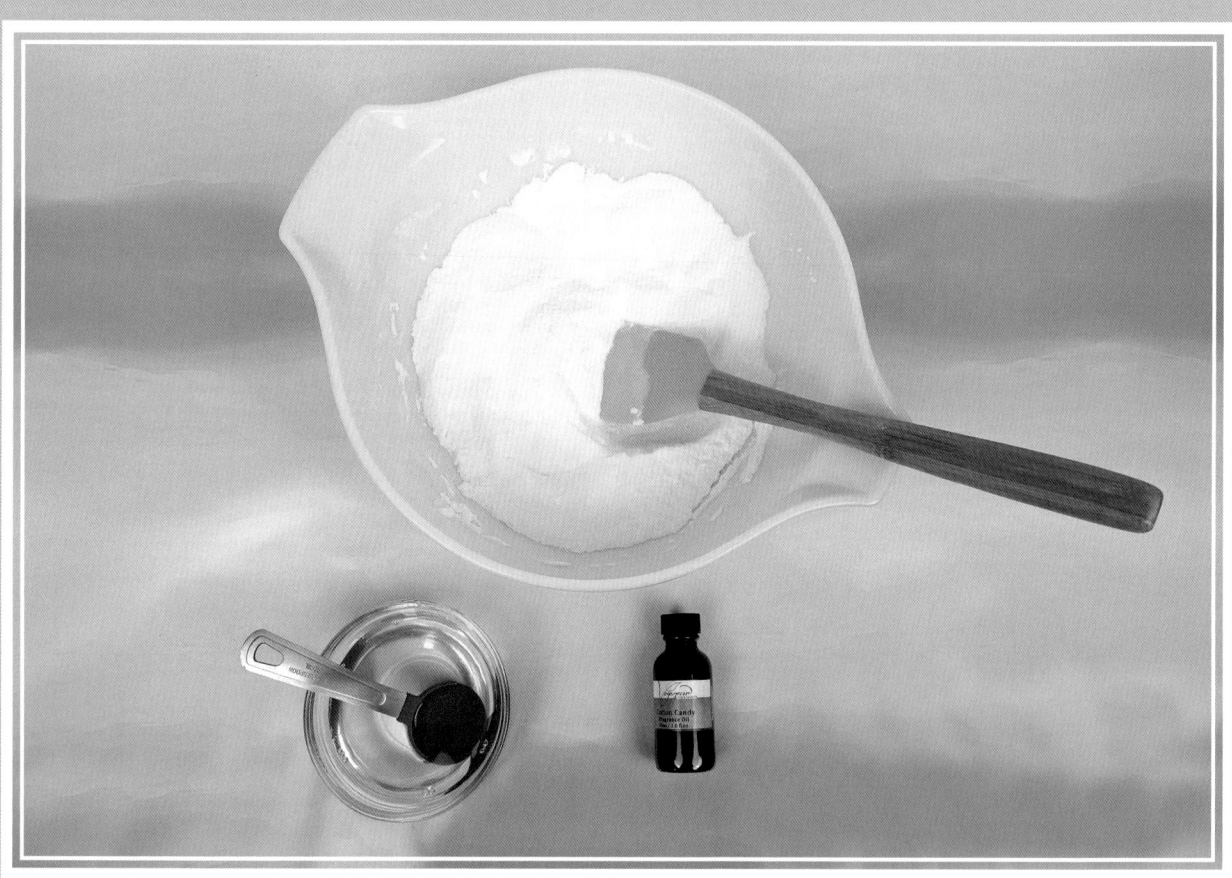

Step 1

Instructions:

Step 1: In a large bowl, combine baking soda, Epsom salt, citric acid, and cornstarch. Stir to thoroughly mix ingredients together.

Step 2: Add fragrance oil to the bowl of ingredients. Then add coconut oil 1 tablespoon at a time, mixing before adding more. You want your bath bomb mixture to have the consistency of damp sand. It should pack together when you form it into a ball between your hands. If the bath bomb mixture is falling apart, add more melted coconut oil.

Step 3: Use meatball tongs, bath bomb molds, or silicone soap molds to make your bath bombs. You want to tightly pack the bath bomb mixture into the tool you are shaping it with. When using meatball tongs, I carefully remove the bath bomb and set it on a plate to dry overnight. If using a silicone soap mold, you can leave the bath bomb mixture in the mold to dry overnight.

Step 4: Once your bath bombs dry and you have removed them from the mold, you now get to decorate them. Mix ½ teaspoon of each color of mica powder you would like to use with 1 teaspoon of isopropyl alcohol to create a paint. Use your paintbrush to paint the caticorns' horn, eyes, ears, and mouth.

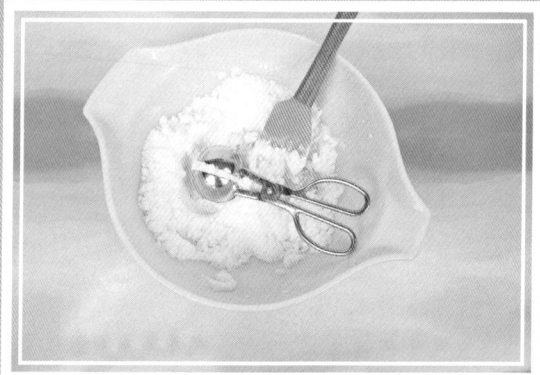

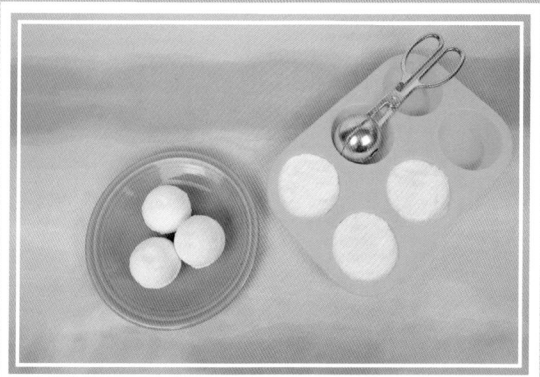

🐾 **Pro Crafter Tip** 🐾

Your "paint" will dry up as the alcohol evaporates. Add more alcohol as needed to refresh your paint and thin out the mica powder. Save the mica powder when you're done, and the next time you make bath bombs, add more alcohol for a fresh batch of bath bomb paint!

Store bath bombs in an airtight container until ready to use. Drop a bath bomb into your bath, and float away on a cotton candy caticorn–scented breeze!

Purr-ty Painted Caticorn Rocks

One of my friends started a group called Rock Art Canada in which members paint rocks and leave them in public places. She paints rocks with different themes and leaves them in parks and playgrounds, at fun family places like the aquarium and science center, and at places where people might need a bit of cheer like the Ronald McDonald House, children's hospitals, and retirement homes. I love the movement that she has created and knew that I wanted to do a set of caticorn-themed rocks for this book. I hope that this project encourages you to paint rocks of your own and leave them out for other people to discover and enjoy!

Materials:

- Rocks (Find these at the ocean, in the forest, by the river, or at your local craft or garden store)
- Spray paint in any color you'd like
- Pencil
- Paintbrushes
- Acrylic paint
- Paint pens
- Clear spray paint for sealing

Note: I used paint pens for this project because I love the control that I can get with them; however, they aren't as opaque as acrylic paint, so I did a layer of white acrylic paint first and then painted over it. My friend paints all of her rocks with acrylic paint and paintbrushes.

Step 1: Wash your rocks and allow them to dry. You should have a nice blank canvas to work on, so I suggest spraying a layer of clear spray paint, colored spray paint, or even laying down a layer of acrylic paint. Allow to thoroughly dry.

Step 2: Sketch out your caticorn drawing with a pencil. I then "colored in" my drawing with acrylic paint.

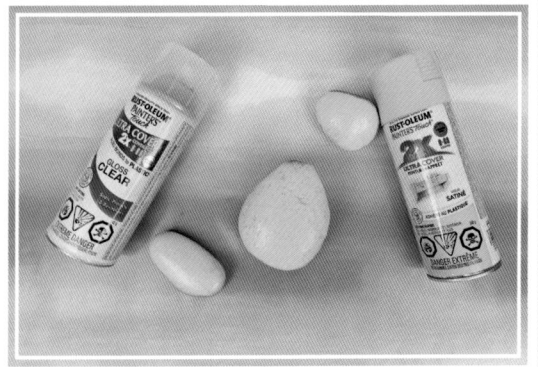

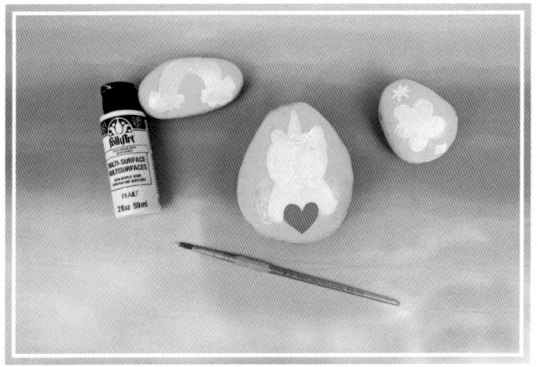

Step 3: Add finer details like the horn, eyes, centers of the ears, etc. using your paint pens.

Step 4: Spray with clear spray paint to seal your rocks.

Place rocks in your garden, use as a paperweight on your desk, or hide in your community for others to find!

🐾 **Pro Crafter Tip** 🐾

The sky is the limit with painted rocks! If drawing isn't your strength, try decorating them with temporary tattoos and then sealing with clear spray paint!

Meowgical

Smitten Kitten Ombre Caticorn Picture Frame

I have a "thing" for stickers! When I was a kid, I used to buy them, trade them, and collect them in a sticker book. Now as an adult, I love to design my own and print them on printable sticker paper! I'm always looking for fun new places to adhere my stickers. I like to find places where I get to see my stickers all the time, like on a picture frame! For this project, we're going to use a simple wood picture frame that you can find in the wood aisle at your favorite craft store, give it an ombre-style paint job, and decorate it with a pretty caticorn sticker. You can either draw your own caticorn for your sticker, or use the template that I have in the back of this book!

Materials:

- Acrylic paint in your favorite color
- An old plate or another surface to mix paint on
- Foam brush
- Wood picture frame
- White acrylic paint
- Sandpaper
- Printer
- Printable sticker paper or printable vinyl
- Scissors

Instructions:

Step 1: Squirt a bit of your favorite color of paint on a plate. Dip your foam brush in the paint, and paint a stripe along the bottom of your wood picture frame.

Add a drop or two of white paint to the paint on your plate. Mix together with your brush, and paint another stripe on your picture frame, slightly overlapping your first stripe.

Add another drop or two of white paint to the paint on your plate. Mix together with your brush, and paint another stripe on your picture frame, slightly overlapping your second stripe. Repeat this process until your entire picture frame is covered. Set aside to dry.

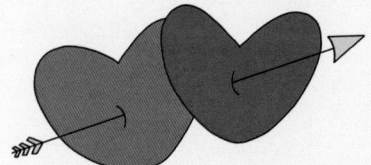

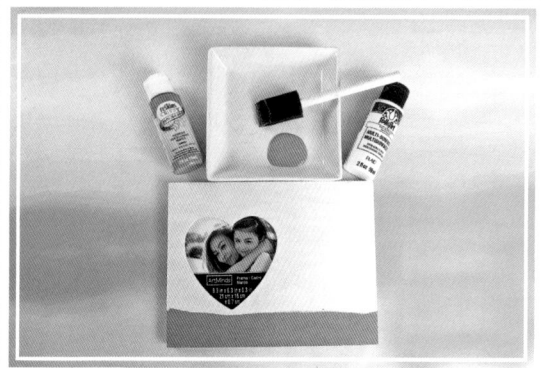

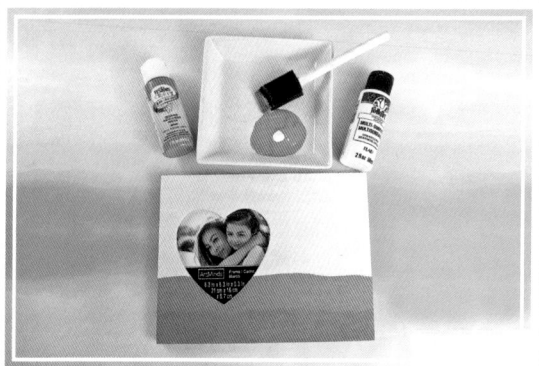

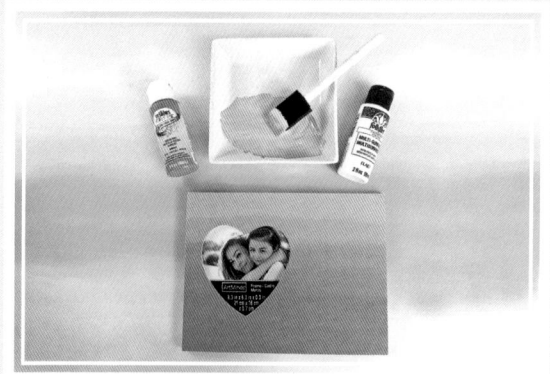

Step 2: Once paint has dried, use your sandpaper to lightly sand your picture frame. This helps blend any obvious lines between paint colors.

Step 3: Scan the caticorn image at the back of this book, and print it out on printable sticker paper. With your scissors, cut around the caticorn, staying as close to the outline as possible.

Step 4: Peel the paper backing from the back of your sticker paper, and position your sticker on your picture frame. Put your favorite photo in your picture frame and display it for all to see!

🐾 **Pro Crafter Tip** 🐾

Find inexpensive wood photo frames with fun shapes like the heart one that I used for this project in the wood aisle of your local craft store!

SLEEPY KITTY NO-SEW SLEEP MASK

Rest your sleepy head on your Caticorn Pillow from page 7 of this book and drift off to dreamland with this beautiful no-sew sleep mask! I love making quick and easy projects with no special equipment, and this sleep mask is just that! We're using fleece for the mask (because it feels soft on the eyes), felt to decorate (because we love all the fun colors), and fabric glue to hold it all together (because then you don't have to pull out the sewing machine!).

Materials:

- 🐾 Tracing paper
- 🐾 White fleece
- 🐾 Scissors
- 🐾 Felt in black and rainbow colors
- 🐾 Tacky glue or fabric glue
- 🐾 Elastic
- 🐾 Ruler
- 🐾 Optional: hole punch

Instructions:

Step 1: Use the template in the back of this book to trace the pattern pieces for the sleep mask onto tracing paper. Cut each piece out and then use the pattern pieces to cut two face mask pieces out of white fleece and the eyes, nose, inner ears, horn, flowers, and whisker dots out of felt.

Step 2: Glue each felt piece to the front of one of your fleece sleep mask pieces.

Step 3: Cut a piece of elastic so that it is 11 inches long.

🐾 **Pro Crafter Tip** 🐾
Use a hole punch to punch black circles for the whisker dots.

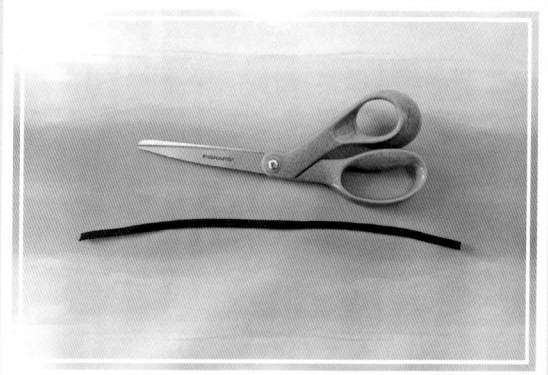

Step 4: Apply glue to the back piece of your sleep mask, paying close attention to the outer edges of the mask. Lay your sleep mask on top of the elastic and turn in each end of the elastic so that it is centered on the sleep mask and secured in the glue.

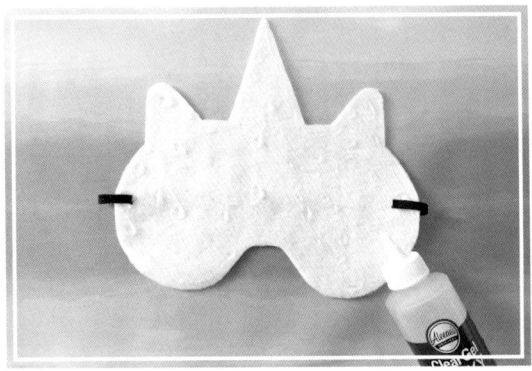

Step 5: Carefully lay your top piece of the face mask onto the bottom piece of the face mask, making sure to line up all of the edges. Line up the top of the horn on your front and back piece of the sleep mask. Once you are sure all edges are lined up, press down on the top of the sleep mask and examine all of the edges to ensure they are all glued shut. You may want to sneak an extra drop of glue in where the elastic is sandwiched between the two pieces of fleece.

Step 6: Allow your glue to dry for 24 hours. If there are any edges that don't quite line up, trim with your scissors. Wear your new Sleepy Kitty Caticorn Sleep Mask and have sweet dreams!

🐾 Pro Crafter Tip 🐾

I purposefully created this sleep mask as a no-sew project so that anyone can make it. However, if you would like to give the elastic a bit more strength, you can sew all the way around the outside edges of your sleep mask using a $1/8$-inch seam allowance.

Caticorn Wrapped Present

I LOVE giving handmade gifts. Even when I'm giving a store-bought present, I love adding a handmade element to the gift I am giving. Sometimes adding a handmade touch to a present can be as simple as creating a bit of DIY wrapping paper, which is exactly what we are doing with this project! We're wrapping it up caticorn style!

Materials:

- Plain colored paper (you can use craft paper, butcher paper, wrapping paper, or even copier paper)
- Scissors
- Tape
- Glitter paper (or whatever kind of paper you want to use for the horn)
- Glue gun and glue
- Markers
- Any embellishments you want to add to your gift like felt or paper flowers, sequins, yarn, or glitter

Instructions:

Step 1: Cut a piece of paper big enough to wrap your present. Wrap the paper around your gift, taping in the back. Fold the wrapping paper at the bottom of the gift and tape.

For the top of the gift, fold the front and back parts of the wrapping paper down and tape into place, leaving triangle flaps sticking up on the right and the left side of the package. These will be your caticorn's ears.

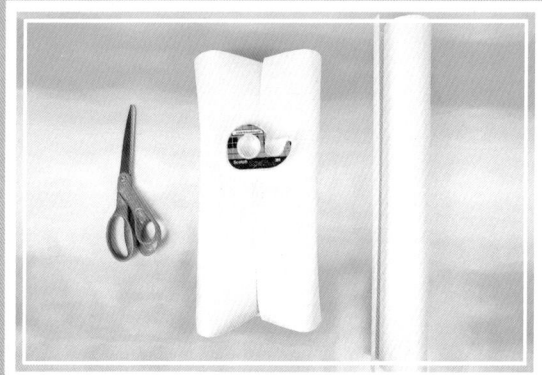

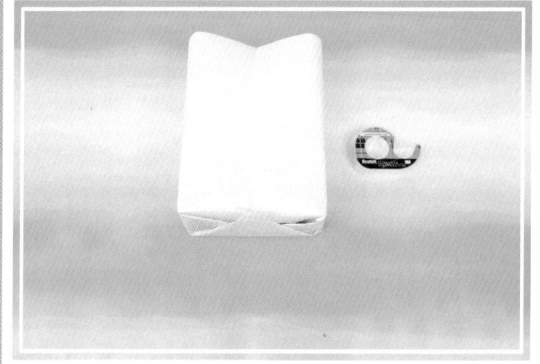

Step 2: Create a horn out of your glitter paper using the template in the back of this book. Use your glue gun to glue the horn to the top of the package between the two ears.

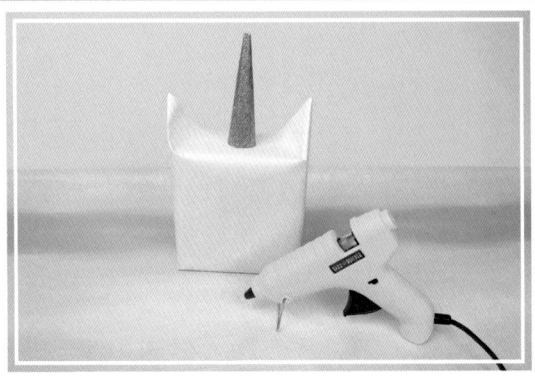

Step 3: Use markers to create an adorable kitty face for your caticorn.

Step 4: Decorate your package with any additional embellishments that you would like to add like flowers and sequins.

Give your caticorn-wrapped present to a friend or loved one! We guarantee that your package will be the cutest on the table!

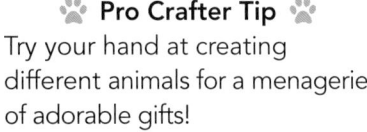

🐾 **Pro Crafter Tip** 🐾
Try your hand at creating different animals for a menagerie of adorable gifts!

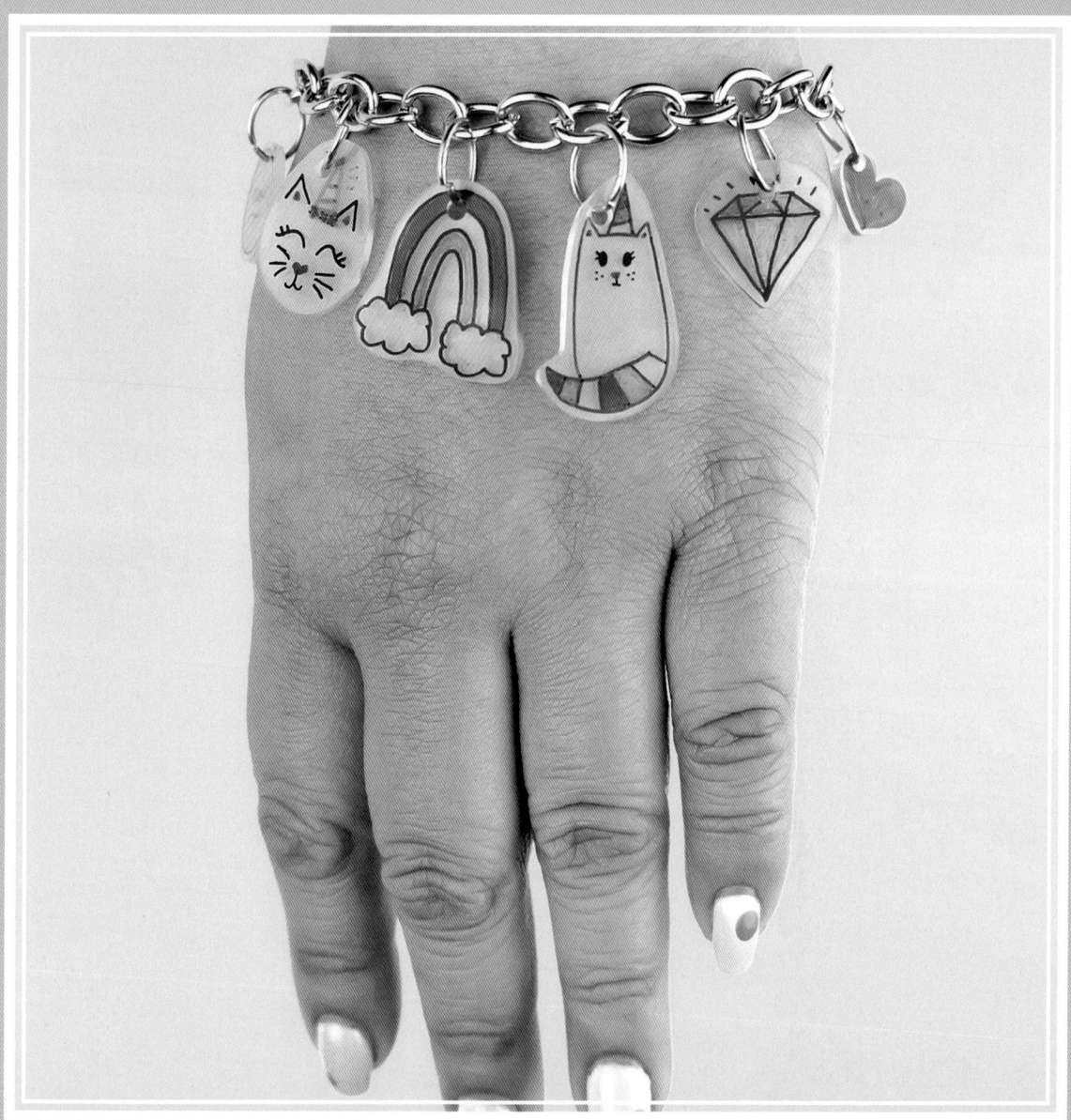

Groovy Kitty Caticorn Charm Bracelet

As a tween, I collected two things: unicorns and charms for my charm bracelet. As I wrote *Caticorn Crafts* and created each of the projects in this book, I kept thinking to myself, "My teenage self would be so excited and would never believe that she grew up to write a book about caticorns." This project is the perfect combination of things that I loved as a child. I love how it turned out so much and am so excited about the idea of these Meowgical bracelets dangling from the wrists of caticorn lovers everywhere.

Materials:

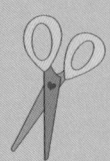

- Permanent markers (I used Sharpies)
- Clear Shrinky Dink plastic
- White paper
- Scissors
- Hole punch
- Baking sheet lined with tin foil or parchment paper
- Oven or toaster oven
- Jewelry pliers
- Charm bracelet (you can find this in the jewelry-making section of your local craft store)
- Jump rings

Instructions:

Step 1: Using a permanent marker, draw the shapes that you would like for your charm bracelet on a sheet of Shrinky Dink plastic. Shrinky Dinks shrink down to one-third their size. I find that 1 inch to 1½ inches shrinks down to the perfect size for charms. Make sure you leave lots of room around each design so you can cut them out. Keep in mind that the colors you use for your drawings will get darker after you put them in the oven. I like to fill my page with more designs than I plan on using for my bracelet so that I have a lot to choose from. I like to put a piece of white paper under my Shrinky Dink sheet so it's easy to see what I am drawing.

🐾 **Pro Crafter Tip** 🐾
Made a mistake on your Shrinky Dink Sheet? No problem! Put a bit of rubbing alcohol onto a paper towel and wipe your design away and start fresh!

Step 2: Use your scissors to cut out your designs.

Step 3: Use a hole punch to punch a hole in each design. This is where your jump ring will loop through to attach your charm to your charm bracelet.

Step 4: Lay your Shrinky Dink designs on a baking sheet lined with foil or parchment paper. Bake in your oven or toaster oven following the instructions on your Shrinky Dink packaging.

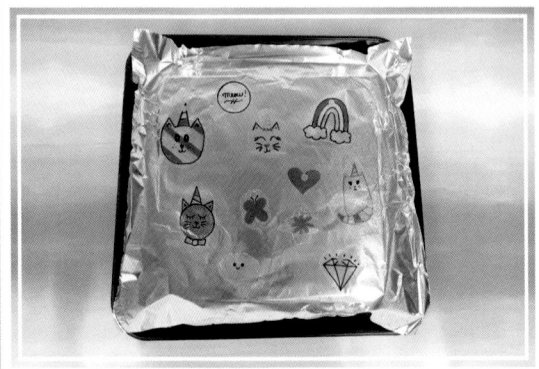

Step 5: Decide which charms you're going to use for your bracelet and lay them out in the order you'll put them on your charm bracelet.

Step 6: Loop a jump ring through the hole on each charm and attach it to your charm bracelet using your jewelry pliers.

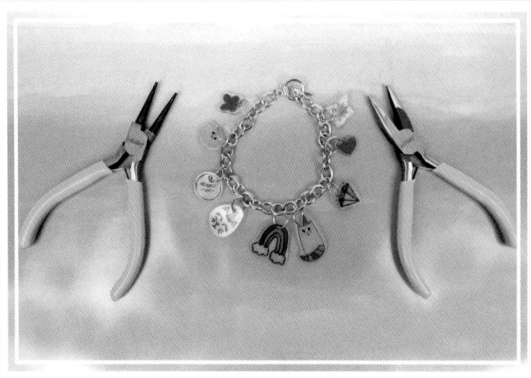

Enjoy the beautiful bracelet that you made!

🐾 Pro Crafter Tip 🐾
If drawing isn't your strength, don't let that hold you back from making this project! Search for caticorn images online, print them out, trace them onto Shrinky Dink sheets, and then color them in!

DIY Rainbow Popsicle Stick Letterboard Sign

One of the hottest Instagram trends from the past year has been pretty letterboard signs. With this project, we're going to DIY our own pretty little colorful sign using Popsicle sticks! I've painted mine with gorgeous rainbow colors that will brighten any space. Use the DIY Caticorn Letterboard Artwork project on page 69 of this book to make your very own caticorn to decorate your DIY letterboard!

Materials:

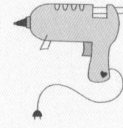

- Paint in rainbow colors
- Foam brushes
- 11 Popsicle sticks (you may need more or less depending on the length and width of your Popsicle sticks)
- Glue and glue gun
- Scissors

Instructions:

Step 1: Paint 8 of your Popsicle sticks in your favorite rainbow colors and allow to dry. You may want to add a second or third coat of paint to your Popsicle sticks depending on how intense you want the colors.

Step 2: Lay two of your unpainted Popsicle sticks side by side to act as support for the backing. Use your glue gun to glue the painted Popsicle sticks to the unpainted Popsicle sticks. Make sure to leave a bit of space between each painted stick so there's room for the pegs of your letterboard letters to fit in between.

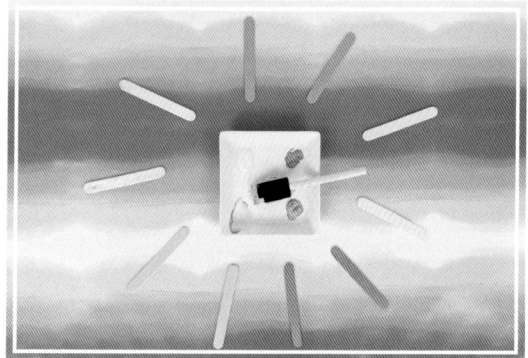

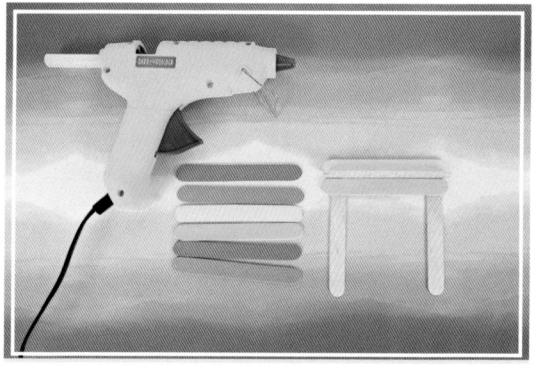

🐾 **Pro Crafter Tip** 🐾
Use the side of an extra Popsicle stick as a spacer when gluing down each Popsicle stick.

Step 3: Once you have all of your Popsicle sticks glued down, flip over your letterboard. Cut your last Popsicle stick in half and glue it at an angle to the back of your letterboard to act as a stand (like you would see on the back of a picture frame).

Decorate with letterboard letters and DIY Caticorn Letterboard Artwork from page 69 of this book! Use it to decorate your dresser, desk, or any other place where you want a burst of colorful happiness!

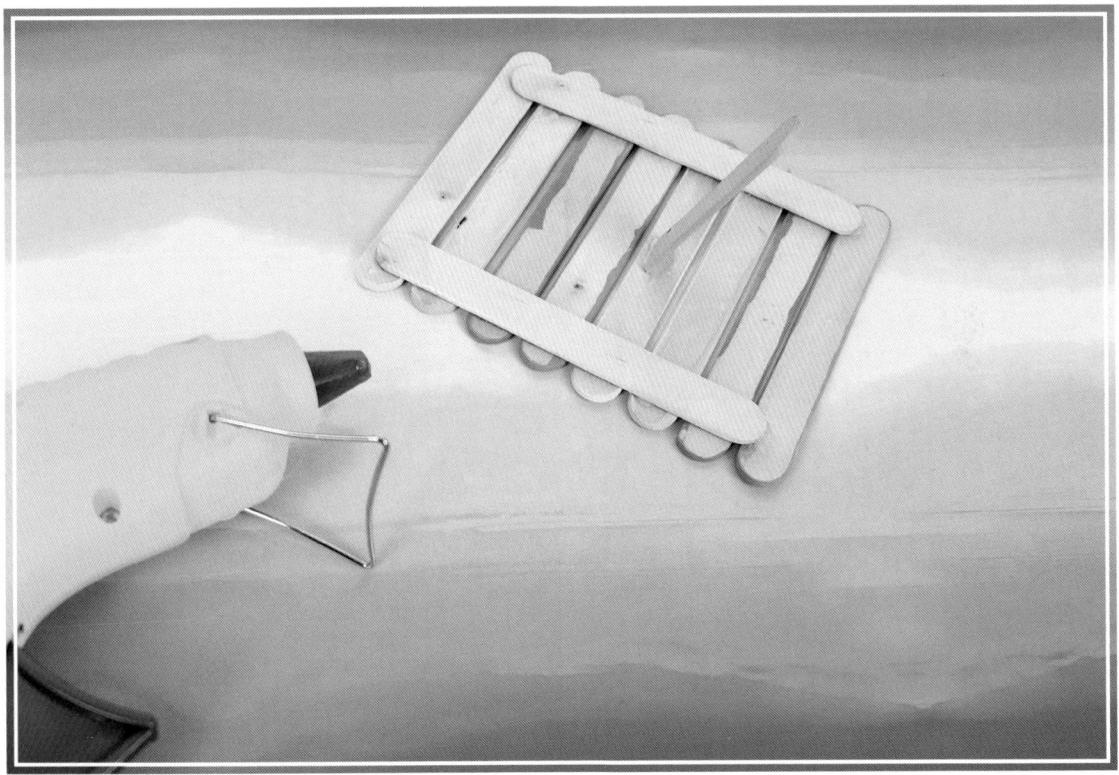

CURL UP WITH A GOOD BOOK CATICORN PAGE CORNER BOOKMARKS

This magical little craft combines three of my favorite things: crafting, caticorns, and reading! Corner bookmarks are a quick and easy little craft project that involves easy origami! Once you have these simple folds down, you'll be making corner bookmarks all the time. Use the templates in the back of this book to decorate your caticorn with our horn, nose, ears, and wings or make yours 100 percent unique by drawing them yourself!

A note on supplies: The double-sided adhesive foam squares that I recommend in this project make attaching the different pieces of this projects quick, easy, permanent, and instantly dry but if you don't have any, a glue stick or liquid glue can work too!

Materials:

- A square piece of paper in your favorite color
- Plain and glitter card stock (We used gold for the horn, pink for the nose and inner ears, and blue for the wings)
- Scissors
- Glue (Whatever you like for gluing paper is great! Liquid glue or a glue stick)
- Double-sided adhesive foam squares
- Pens or markers for decorating the face

Instructions:

To fold your bookmark:

Step 1: Lay your square piece of paper so that one corner of the square is pointed toward you and the other is pointed away from you.

Step 2: Fold up the bottom corner of your square to meet the top corner of your square to make a triangle.

Step 3: Fold up the left corner of the triangle so it meets the top corner of the triangle.

Step 4: Fold up the right corner of the triangle so it meets the top corner of the triangle.

Step 5: Open your triangle so the fold of the triangle is closest to you and the point of the triangle is pointed away from you.

Step 6: Fold down the top corner of your triangle toward you so that the point meets the center of the bottom fold.

Step 7: Take the left corner of your triangle and tuck it into the little pocket you've just created, pushing the corner all the way to the bottom so that your fold lines up with the top of the pocket.

Step 8: Repeat step 7 with the right corner.

Yay! You have a corner bookmark! Now let's decorate it!

Decorating your bookmark:

Step 1: Use the templates in the back of the book (or your imagination) to cut caticorn pieces out of plain and glitter card stock.

Step 2: Use a glue stick, liquid glue, or adhesive foam squares to attach each caticorn piece to your corner bookmark.

If using a glue stick or liquid glue, press your pieces under a heavy book and allow to dry before proceeding to the next step.

Step 3: Use a pen to add eyes, whiskers, and any other pieces of caticorn personality you'd like on your bookmark!

Now, curl up with a good book and mark your place with your pretty new corner bookmark!

Sleepy Kitty Caticorn Dream Catcher

This project is my colorful and whimsical twist on a dream catcher! Also referred to as Sacred Hoops, dream catchers were traditionally used as talismans to protect sleeping children from bad dreams and nightmares. Hang your Sleepy Kitty Caticorn Dream Catcher on your wall, close your eyes, and be transported somewhere over the rainbow! You'll have nothing but sweet dreams with this pretty craft!

Materials:

- Embroidery hoop
- Yarn
- Glue gun and glue gun glue sticks
- Scissors
- Felt
- Ribbon, rickrack, and other pretty treasures to embellish your dream catcher
- Optional: Extra embellishments like felt or paper flowers, glitter, etc.

Instructions:

Step 1: First we are going to disguise the embroidery hoop by wrapping it in yarn. Use a glue gun to attach one end of the yarn to the top of the embroidery hoop. Wrap the yarn around and around the hoop, pushing each loop so it's tightly against the loop before working all the way around the embroidery hoop circle. When you get back to the top of the embroidery hoop cut your yarn and secure it with a drop of glue from your glue gun.

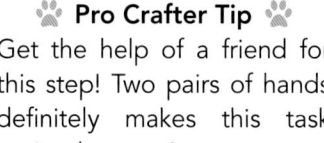

🐾 **Pro Crafter Tip** 🐾

Get the help of a friend for this step! Two pairs of hands definitely makes this task easier than one!

Step 2: Tie your yarn to the embroidery hoop, and then crisscross it back and forth across your hoop, pulling tight. When you've created the look you want for your dream catcher, tie the end of the yarn to the embroidery hoop and then trim the ends of the yarn.

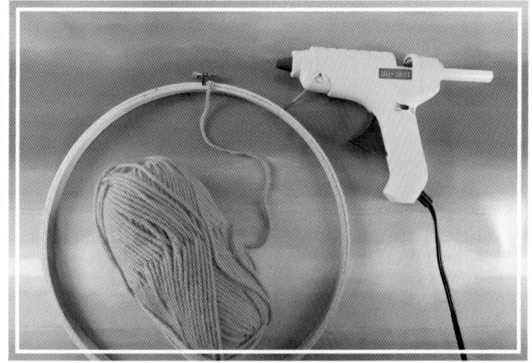

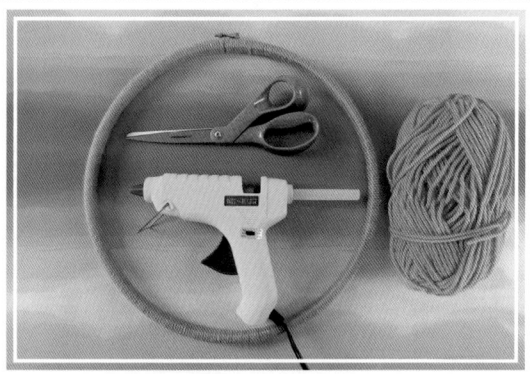

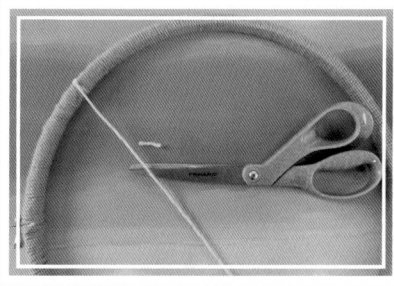

Step 3: Cut caticorn's ears, eyes, horn, mouth, and nose out of felt, and then use hot glue to attach them to the yarn and embroidery hoop of the dream catcher.

Step 4: Loop a piece of ribbon, yarn, or rickrack through the hanger at the top of the embroidery hoop and tie (or glue). This will allow you to hang your dream catcher.

Step 5: Cut ribbon, yarn, and rickrack to various lengths and tie it to the bottom of your dream catcher.

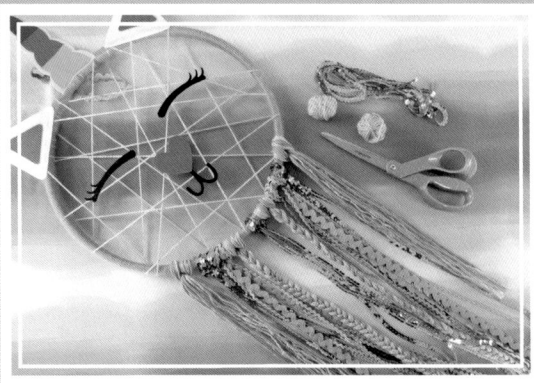

Optional Step: Embellish with "extras" like felt or paper flowers, glitter, etc.

Hang on the wall in your bedroom and have magical caticorn dreams!

DIY Caticorn Letterboard Artwork

On page 55 of this book, we taught you how to make a DIY Rainbow Popsicle Stick Letterboard Sign! In this project, we're going to make pretty letterboard artwork to decorate any letterboard with! Once you know how to make your own letterboard artwork, I know you'll come up with all kinds of inspirational sayings and artwork to decorate your letterboard with!

Materials:

- Drawing supplies and/or a printer
- Printable sticker paper
- Craft knife
- Card stock in your favorite color
- Scissors
- Plastic (we used plastic from some packaging that we were going to throw into recycling)
- Glue and glue gun
- Letterboard

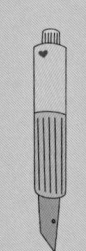
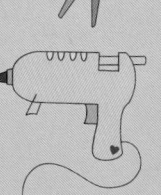

Instructions:

Step 1: Draw your saying and caticorn on a piece of printable sticker paper or copy the images we used for our project from the templates section of this book. Use your craft knife to cut around your images. Peel the excess sticker paper off of your sheet, leaving your stickers on the paper.

Step 2: Place your stickers onto card stock and make sure to leave lots of room around each sticker.

Step 3: Use your scissors either to cut around each sticker, leaving a colored border like we did with our words, or to cut right next to the image like we did with our caticorn.

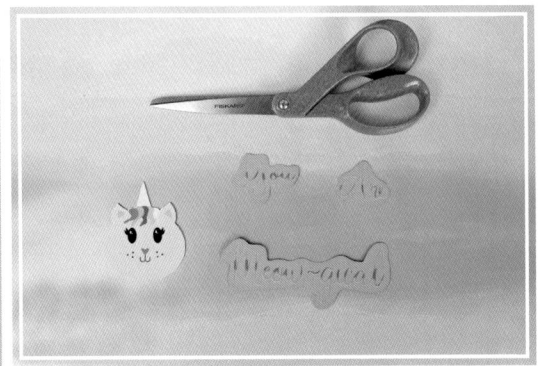

Step 4: Cut small strips of plastic and fold them in half. These are going to be what hold your words and image to your letterboard, so you'll want to check that they fit properly into the slats of your letterboard.

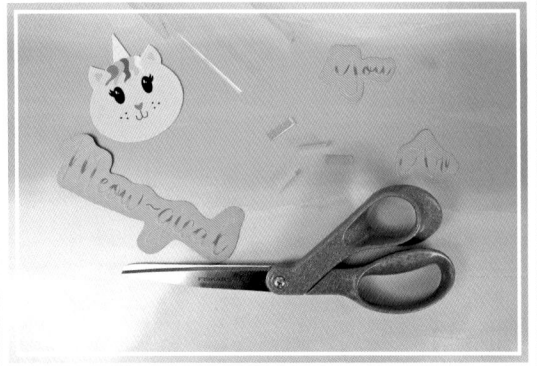

Step 5: Use your glue gun to glue the plastic pieces to the back of your letterboard artwork. Leave to dry until the glue has cooled and hardened.

Step 6: Put your artwork on your letterboard as a constant reminder that you are Meowgical!

Step 6

Unicorn Kitty Painted Mason Jar

A crafter can never have too many cups, jars, and holders in their craft space to put all their pens, pencils, markers, brushes, and other doodads! A few years ago, I started a collection of handmade animal-shaped "holders" for my craft room table to organize all my craft tools. My collection includes a sloth, polar bear, penguin, and panda-corn. As soon as I started writing this book, I knew I had to add a unicorn kitty to my menagerie! I hope you make one, too, and that she helps you with your craft room organization!

Materials:

- Mason jar
- Clear spray paint
- Acrylic paint in your favorite unicorn kitty color
- Foam brush
- Scissors
- Felt
- Sparkle card stock
- Glue and/or glue gun and glue sticks
- Pencil
- Paint pens
- Embellishments like flowers and sequins to decorate your unicorn kitty

Instructions:

Step 1: In a well-ventilated area, spray the outside of your mason jar with a layer of clear spray paint. Leave to dry.

Step 2: Paint the outside of your mason jar with acrylic paint using a foam brush. You may need to apply a few layers to achieve your desired opacity. Allow paint to dry between each layer.

🐾 **Pro Crafter Tip** 🐾

The reason we spray the mason jar with spray paint is to prime the glass for paint. The paint will go onto the glass so much easier over a layer of spray paint.

🐾 **Pro Crafter Tip** 🐾

Switch the direction that you paint in for each layer of paint. Paint horizontal for one layer and then vertical for the next.

Step 3: Cut ears out of felt and a horn out of sparkle card stock and then glue them to your mason jar using your glue gun. Use a pencil to very lightly draw your unicorn kitty's face on your mason jar.

Step 4: Use your paint pens to go over your pencil lines and color in your unicorn kitty's face.

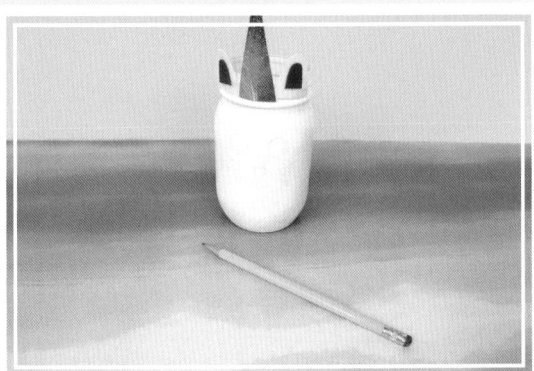

Step 5: Add embellishments to your unicorn kitty. You might want to add a collar of sequins and a flower crown.

Step 6: Fill with pens, pencils, markers, crafting tools, or flowers and use to brighten any space!

Strike A Purr-ty Pose Caticorn Masquerade Mask

Strike your purr-fect caticorn pose with these glittery gorgeous masquerade masks! This project is super fun because your mask can be as simple or as fancy as you want it! Start by making a simple caticorn mask using scissors, card stock, glue, and a chopstick, and then decorate it as fancy as you want using markers, glitter, sequins, yarn, paper flowers, or more! These masquerade masks would be a ton of fun for a photo booth at a caticorn birthday party or even for striking poses in front of your mirror!

Materials:
- Pencil
- Card stock in your favorite caticorn color
- Scissors
- Marker
- Glue gun and glue
- Chopstick

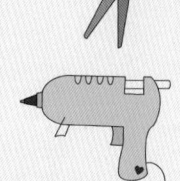

Optional Materials:
- Paint
- Foam Brushes
- Mod Podge or Glue
- Glitter
- Sequins
- Yarn
- Paper flowers

Instructions:

Step 1: Use the masquerade mask template in the back of this book to trace and then cut your masquerade mask out of card stock.

Optional: Make your masquerade mask extra creative by decorating the mask and chopstick with glitter, sequins, paint, yarn, and other embellishments.

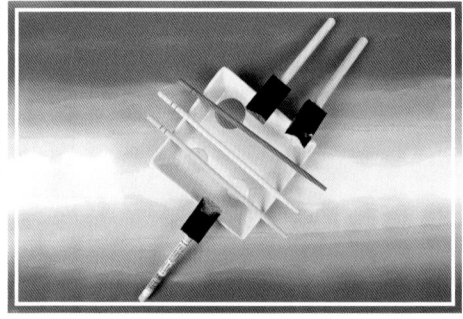

Step 2: Decorate your mask using markers.

Step 3: Use your glue gun to glue the chopstick to the back of the sleep mask. Strike a purr-ty pose and snap a picture!

🐾 Pro Crafter Tip 🐾
Love glitter? So do I! It's easy to glitter just about anything! Add a thin layer of glue to a project, sprinkle glitter on top, tap away the excess, and then leave to dry!

Hungry Kitty Caticorn Lunch Bag

When I was a little girl, my mom used to draw pictures on the outside of my brown paper lunch bag. Each day my classmates would gather around and see what kind of art she'd left me that day. It made me feel so special to know that my mom had taken the time to create something handmade for me. Since caticorns are all about spreading love and magic, it seemed appropriate to include a project like this in the book. These Hungry Kitty Caticorn Lunch Bags will only take you a couple of minutes to make and require basic materials that you probably already have lying around the house! Send them to school packed with lunch or snacks to brighten someone's day! They'd also be supercute for a unicorn kitty–themed birthday party either as a favor bag or filled with popcorn for a snack!

Materials:

- Paper lunch bags
- Pencil
- Scissors
- Markers

Instructions:

Step 1: Using your pencil, trace your caticorn's ears and horn onto your paper bag.

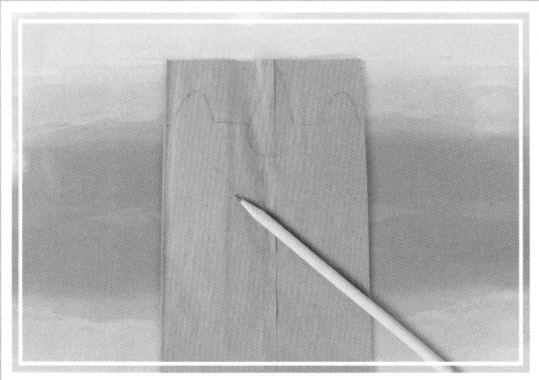

Step 2: Using your scissors, cut out the ears and the horn following the lines you just drew.

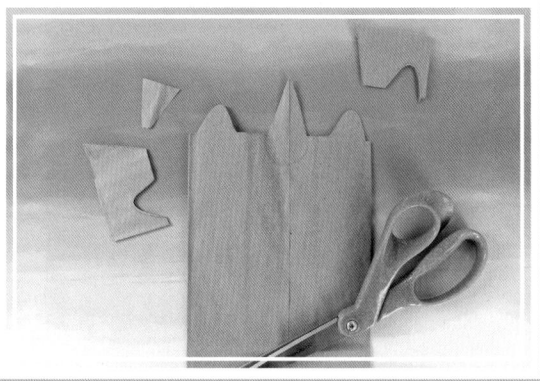

Step 3: Color in your caticorn using brightly colored markers!

Fill your Hungry Kitty Caticorn Lunch Bag with delicious snacks and spread a bit of happiness and magic to those around you!

Step 3

Meowgical Caticorn Paper Lantern

When I first started dreaming up the caticorn crafts for this book, this project wasn't on my list. Then one day, I was browsing the aisles of my local craft store and started thinking about all the things that could be used to decorate a caticorn-themed room. I had a caticorn throw pillow for the bed, a caticorn pencil holder for the desk, a caticorn dream catcher to hang on the wall, a caticorn corner bookmark for marking the pages in a book—but what about a light to read by? Just then I walked past the store's wedding section and the pretty paper lanterns caught my eye. They seemed like the purr-fect blank canvas for "caticorning" on, and so this project was born! I hope you love it as much as I do!

Materials:

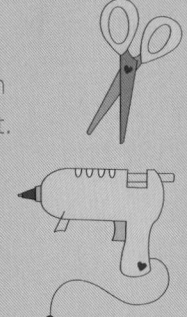

- Scissors
- Felt
- Styrofoam unicorn horn (Ours is from FloraCraft. Alternatively you could also use paper rolled into a cone or felt)
- Paint or markers
- Glue
- Glitter
- Glue gun and glue sticks

Instructions:

Step 1: Cut out ears, eyes, nose, mouth, hair, and cheeks for caticorn from felt.

Step 2: Color your Styrofoam horn using either paint or markers. Allow to dry, and then apply glue to your horn and sprinkle with glitter. Allow glue to dry and then tap off excess glitter.

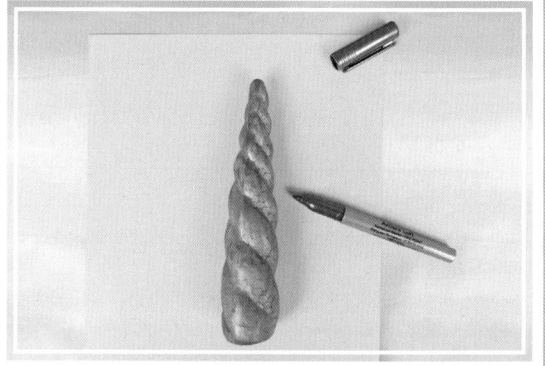

Step 3: While your horn is drying, use your hot glue gun to glue your felt ears to the top of the lantern. I pinched my ears in the middle at the bottom, and glued where I pinched to give the ears a more dimensional look.

Step 4: Use hot glue to attach the horn, hair, eyes, nose, mouth, and cheeks to the lantern.

Decorate your room with your beautiful caticorn paper lantern and read by its meowgical glow!

Love the Purr-ty Planet Upcycled Caticorn Planter

A caticorn's three favorite things are rainbows, flowers, and saving the planet. This fun upcycled project hits all three of those categories! Made with an empty soda pop bottle, this project is inexpensive and as cute as can be! Leave one on a friend's front doorstep to brighten their day, or use as a centerpiece at a caticorn-themed birthday party!

Materials:

- Sharpies
- Clean 2-liter pop bottle
- Scissors
- Paint
- Foam brush
- Pencil
- An old plate or another surface that you can mix paint on.
- Optional: drill

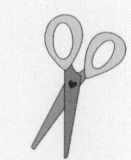
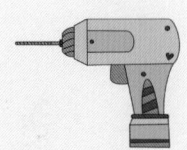

Instructions:

Step 1: Use a Sharpie marker to draw your caticorn's ears, horn, and head on your pop bottle. Line up the center of the face between two of the nubs at the bottom of the bottle so that the nubs will look like legs. I drew the caticorn's head on a piece of paper and used the paper as my template. You can also find a template for this at the back of this book that you can trace.

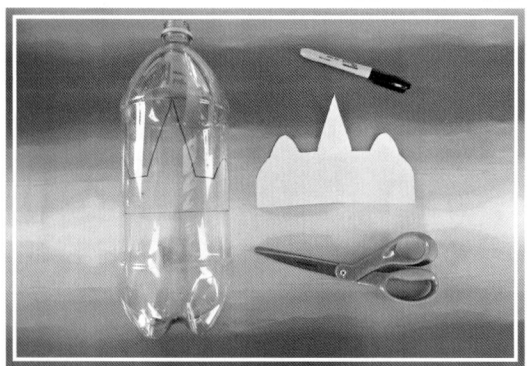

Step 2: Use scissors to cut along the lines you drew on your pop bottle and cut out your caticorn planter.

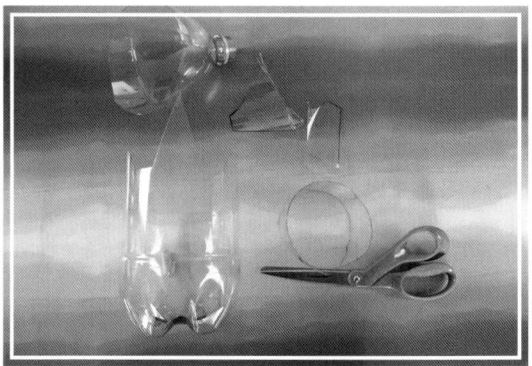

Step 3: Use acrylic craft paint and your foam brush to paint your planter the color you will be using for your caticorn's body. I put three coats of paint on my planters, letting the paint dry before adding the next layer.

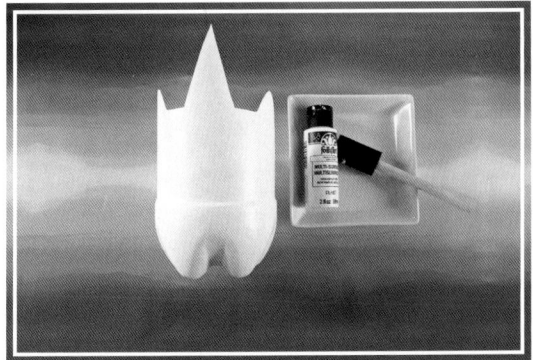

🐾 **Pro Crafter Tip** 🐾

Switch the direction that you apply your paint in for each coat to give a more even, finished look. Paint horizontal for one coat and then vertical for the next coat.

Step 4: Once your final layer of paint has dried, it's time to add the face to your caticorn. I used a pencil to lightly sketch my face before coloring it in with Sharpies. Allow to dry thoroughly.

Optional: Use a drill to create holes in the bottom of your planter for drainage. If you are planning on leaving your planter outside where it can get wet, add a coat of spray sealer to prevent the paint from running.

Now all you have to do is fill your planter with some potting soil and some pretty flowers, and you'll have a beautiful little planter that not only is fun to look at but also eco-friendly!

Caticorns and Confetti Rainbow Popcorn

I love a good party theme! A caticorn birthday just might be the most fun theme under the rainbow! When I think of caticorns, I think of bright colors, sparkles, sweet treats, and fun. This delicious snack checks all those boxes! This popcorn would make a delicious treat at a sleepover or birthday party whether it's a part of a candy bar, served while watching a movie, or sent home in goodie bags. Make sure you check out the Caticorn Popcorn Boxes on page 99 to up the caticorn fun even more!

Materials:

- ½ cup pink candy melts
- ½ cup blue candy melts
- ½ cup yellow candy melts
- Microwave-safe bowls
- 12 cups of plain popped popcorn
- Sheet pan lined with parchment paper
- Spoons
- Tongs
- Rainbow sprinkles

Instructions:

Step 1: Put each color candy melt in their own microwave-safe bowl and melt according to directions on packaging. Be careful when taking the bowls in and out of the microwave! They might be hot! Put popped popcorn onto sheet pan lined with parchment paper.

Step 2: Using a spoon, drizzle melted candy melts onto popcorn. Use tongs to toss popcorn.

Step 3: Add sprinkles to your popcorn. Make sure you do this step before the melted candy hardens.

Set aside for 20 minutes for candy melts to harden and then serve!

🐾 Pro Crafter Tip 🐾

Increase the rainbow fun! The reason I selected pink, blue, and yellow candy melts was because you can use these colors to make other colors of candy melts. Mix pink and blue to make purple, mix blue and yellow to make green, and mix yellow and pink to make orange!

Step 3

Caticorn Popcorn Boxes

No caticorn party is complete without popcorn! Whip up a batch of Caticorns and Confetti Rainbow Popcorn from page 95 of this book and serve it in these party purr-fection caticorn popcorn boxes! These little popcorn boxes would also be supercute as party favor boxes or as a birthday party craft! Give each attendee a popcorn box and set up a table with card stock, scissors, and Glue Dots and see what everyone creates! The caticorn possibilities are endless!

Materials:

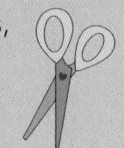

- Card stock for the ears, eyes, nose, mouth, and horn
- Scissors
- Glue Dots and/or glue
- Popcorn box (find these at your favorite party store)

Instructions:

Step 1: Cut out ears, eyes, a nose, mouth, and horn from pretty, colored card stock.

Step 2: Use the Glue Dots or glue to attach the card stock pieces you cut out to your popcorn box! Fill with popcorn and enjoy!

Want to create your own popcorn box from scratch? The template for this project was too large for this book, but visit https://www.hellocreativefamily.com/caticorncrafts for a free printable template.

Step 2

CATICORN POPCORN BOXES **101**

No-Sew Caticorn Cup Cozy

With all the "No-Sew" projects in this book, you might be surprised to learn that I actually *love* to sew. I decided to do no-sew projects for *Caticorn Crafts* because I wanted each of the projects to be easy for anyone to make without needing special equipment. Since making this project, I have slipped it onto my reusable coffee cup at home, and I bring it with me to my local coffee shop whenever I go to get my tea. Each time I use it, I get a ton of smiles and compliments. I love that my cup cozy brightens other people's days. I hope you make one, too, and help to spread the magic!

Materials:

- Cardboard coffee sleeve from your favorite coffee shop to use as a template
- Pencil
- Felt in different colors for the caticorn's face, ears, eyes, nose, and whiskers
- Scissors
- Adhesive velcro
- Glue
- Markers
- Optional: Glue gun and glitter

Instructions:

Step 1: Open a cardboard coffee sleeve from your favorite coffee house and use it as a template. Trace the sleeve onto a piece of felt using a pencil. Once you're done tracing, draw a caticorn horn and ears centered on the top of the sleeve.

Step 2: Use your scissors to follow the lines you drew on the felt and cut out your coffee cozy.

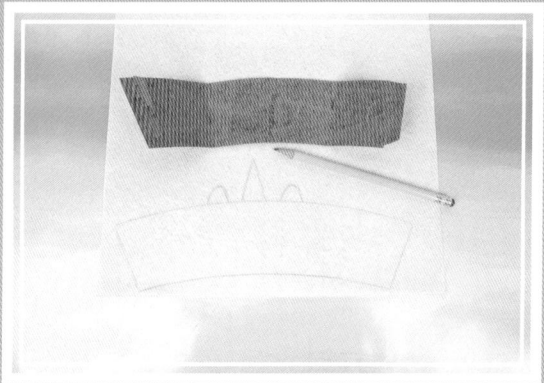

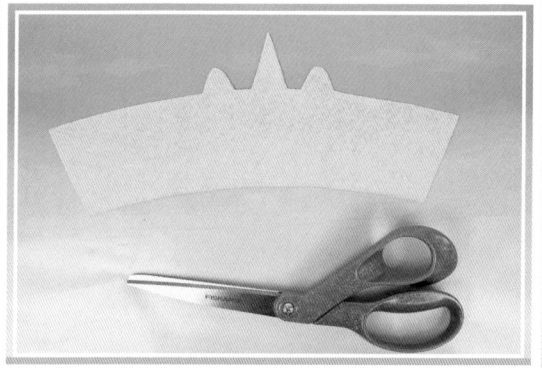

Step 3: Wrap the felt around the cup you want to use your cup cozy with. Place the adhesive velcro on the felt where the ends overlap. If you find that the adhesive isn't sticky enough, place a drop of hot glue on the back of each piece of velcro and restick.

Step 4: Cut center of ears, eyes, nose, and whiskers out of felt.

Step 5: Glue center of ears, eyes, nose, and whiskers to your cup cozy to create a face.

Step 6: Color the horn using markers.

Optional step: Add glue to the horn and sprinkle with glitter. Set aside to dry.

Slip your caticorn cup cozy on your favorite cup and spread the magic everywhere you go!

 **Pro Crafter Tip**
If you spill coffee, tea, or hot chocolate on your cozy, you can spot clean it with a stain remover and a damp cloth!

Optional step

Better than a Ball of Yarn Rainbow Pom-Pom Pencil Toppers

You probably know that cats love to play with balls of yarn, but do you know what a caticorn's favorite toy is? Rainbow pom-poms! In this craft, we're teaching you how to make your very own pop-pom maker and using it to transform a regular pencil into something that's truly Meowgical! Put these pom-pom pencils into the Unicorn Kitty Desktop Pencil Holder from page 13 or the Caticorn Painted Mason Jar from page 75 to create a purr-fect caticorn desk theme!

Materials:

- 🐾 Scissors
- 🐾 A piece of cardboard
- 🐾 Yarn (I love Lion Brand Bon-Bon Yarn)
- 🐾 Pencils
- 🐾 Glue gun and glue gun glue sticks

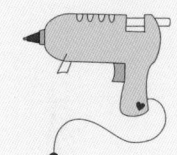

Instructions:

Step 1: Cut a rectangular shape out of a piece of cardboard. Cut a notch going about three-quarters of the way down the center of the length of the cardboard. I think it looks like a pair of pants!

Step 2: Hold the end of your string of yarn against one of the "legs" of your "cardboard pants" and start winding the yarn around and around and around. The way your wrap your yarn will create different patterns in your pom-pom. You can decide whether you want to wrap one color of yarn at a time, make a few layers and then switch to another color of yarn, or if you want to wrap multiple colors of yarn at one time.

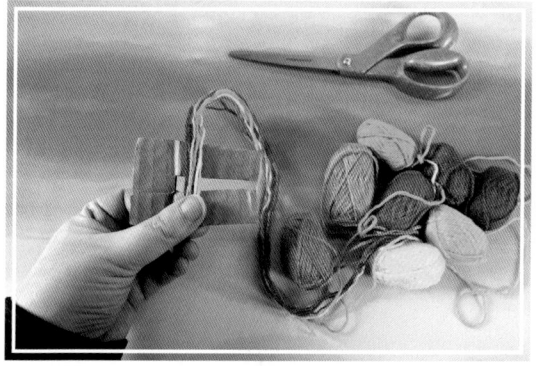

Step 3: Once you are satisfied with the thickness of your pom-pom (I typically wrap it around approximately 25 to 30 times), cut the ends of the yarn. Leave your pom-pom on the cardboard, and tie a piece of yarn tightly around the middle of your pom-pom. Tie several knots to make sure the center band of yarn is tied tightly.

Step 4: Slide your pom-pom off your cardboard pom maker. Use scissors to cut down the center of your looped ends.

Step 5: Now it's time to give your pom-pom a nice haircut to give it a nice, round shape. I like squishing it like a hamburger and cutting a circle around the edges of my pom-pom.

Step 6: Once your pom-pom is in the shape you would like it, it's time to attach it to the pencil! Push your yarn back until you can see the center of your pom-pom. Apply a dollop of glue from your glue gun in the center of the pom-pom, and then stick your pencil eraser into the glue. Hold for a minute or two until your glue dries.

Now you have a super fun rainbow pom-pom pencil topper that any caticorn would have hours of fun playing with!

Step 6

No-Sew Cutie Kitty Caticorn Costume

And here we are at the end of the book! Where did time go? I hope you had fun with all of these projects. I'm leaving you with one of my favorite projects from this collection: the Cutie Kitty Caticorn Costume. My kids love hoodies with fun animal faces on them. This past Halloween, I turned plain old hoodies into giraffe, panda, and parrot costumes. They were so quick and easy to make because I used a glue gun to glue felt pieces onto the hoodie. My kids loved them, and now a year later, they still wear them on a regular basis! When I saw a gray sweatshirt with a rainbow stripe down the sleeve at the store, I knew it had to be turned into a caticorn costume. I'm dedicating this last project in *Caticorn Crafts* to my sweet daughter, Bean, and her rescue uni-puppy Mochi. (Mochi's horn is hidden but he has the sweet, magical heart of a unicorn.) Bean is the exact same age I was when I was at my most unicorn crazy, and it's with her and her friends in mind that I've created each project in this book! I hope that the crafts in this book have brought you as much enjoyment as they have brought me!

Materials:

- Felt for eyes, nose, and whisker dots
- Scissors
- White fleece (or whatever color you would like to use for your horn)
- Fabric markers
- Glue gun and glue gun sticks
- Batting
- Metallic cord
- Hooded sweatshirt
- Optional: Hole punch (I love this for making nice felt circles for my whisker dots) and extra embellishments like fabric flowers for adding extra pizazz!

Instructions:

Step 1: Cut eyes, nose, and whisker dots out of felt. Use the horn template on page X of this book to trace and then cut out the fleece.

Step 2: Color in your horn using fabric markers. Leave to dry.

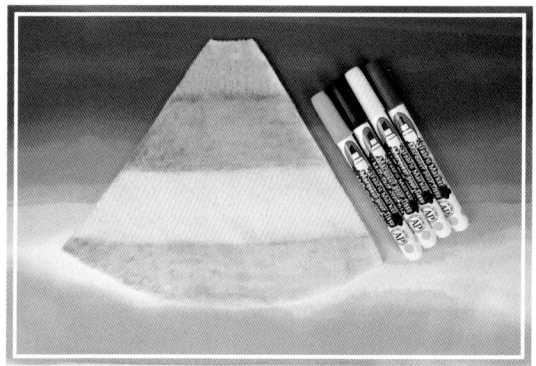

Step 3: Fold your horn and use your glue gun to seal it shut.

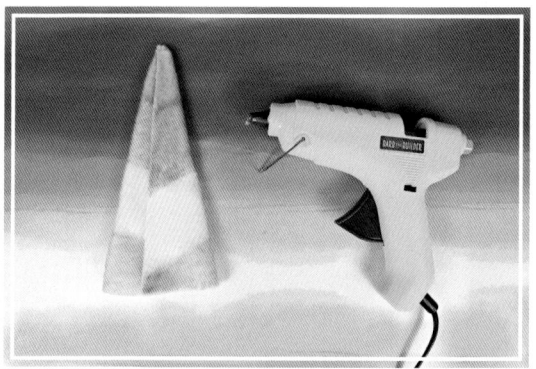

Step 4: Stuff your horn with batting.

Step 5: Glue a piece of fleece to the bottom of your horn to seal the batting inside. Cut the excess fleece away from the base of the horn.

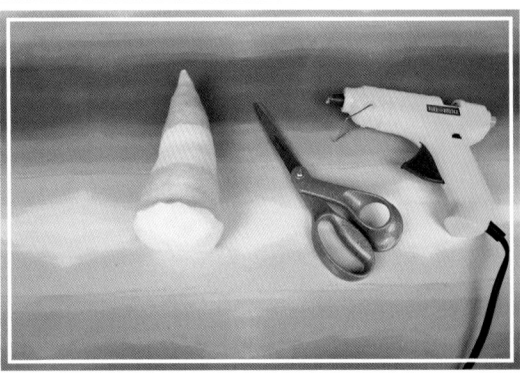

Step 6: Wrap metallic cording around your horn, gluing it with your glue gun at the top and bottom of the horn in the back near the horn seam.

🐾 Pro Crafter Tip 🐾
You might want to use a chopstick to push the batting all the way up into the tip of the horn. Make sure you stuff the horn extra full of batting so it's nice and plump.

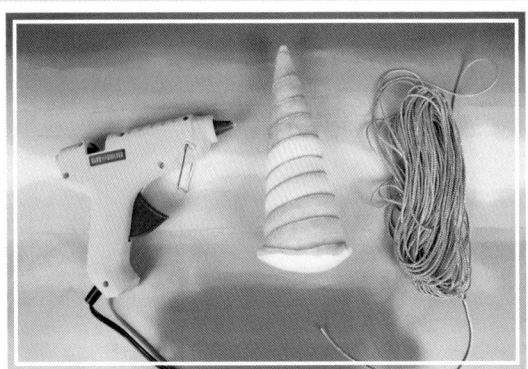

Step 7: Glue the eyes, nose, and whisker dots to the hood of your hooded sweatshirt.

Step 8: Glue the ears and horn to the hood of your sweatshirt.

Step 9: Add pretty embellishments like felt flowers. I think that a strip of sequins around the base of the horn would also be supercute.

Wear your caticorn hoodie out and about and spread the caticorn meow-gic!

🐾 **Pro Crafter Tip** 🐾

I like to have someone wear the hoodie while I'm gluing the horn and the ears on so that I can get the best placement for where the head is going to be in the hood. Be extra careful with the tip of your glue gun and watch out for glue gun drips.

Step 9

Acknowledgments

For the past few months I've been pinching myself each morning, convinced that I'm living in a dreamworld. This is my very first book, and I don't think it could have had a subject matter that is more purr-fect and fun! To all of the caticorn lovers around the world, the reason that this book is in existence is because of you! When I was first approached to write this book, the only caticorns I had seen was the Unikitty™ in the LEGO movies and Pusheen the Cat. As the months have rolled on, I've started to see caticorns everywhere, including in the aisles at my favorite craft stores! That's all because of you and how much you love caticorns! So thank you!

Thank you so much to my editor Nicole Frail for approaching me to write this book. The entire project from contract to completion has been Meowgical thanks to you! I couldn't have asked for a better editor, and I can't wait to get working on our second book together!

The day that Nicole approached me to write this book, I woke to the news that a legend in the book industry had passed away—Allan MacDougall the cofounder and former CEO of Raincoast Books. I worked as a children's book publicist at Raincoast Books for eight years, and Allan was someone who I looked up to, deeply admired, and who I considered a friend. I'll always remember Allan poking his head into my office, asking if I'm busy, and then grabbing a chair to chat about what we'd both been reading. I learned so much not only about the world of children's book publishing, but also about being a good person from Allan, for which I owe him great thanks.

A huge thank-you to my fabulous Hello Creative Family readers. You inspire me so much! Every single day, I say a thank-you to all of you. It's because of your support that I get to live this creative life which is just the most amazing gift.

 To my friend and former business partner, Karen Bannister. Thank you so much for helping me come up with concept of Hello Creative Family, for helping me make the leap to rebrand and for convincing me that leaving my day job to be my own boss would be one of the best decisions I ever made. I miss our lunchtime meetings! Come back!!!

To my blogger bestie Brooke from Brooklyn Berry Designs. Thank you for being my sounding board to bounce ideas off of, for helping to get me back on my game on the days when I have lost my inspiration, and most importantly for being my friend! Thank you also for letting me use some of your supercute drawings in this book. They are purr-fection.

I'm one of those lucky girls who has friends that have become family. Heather, Dunia, Karen, and Tracy: thank you for always having my back, for being my cheerleaders, and for believing in me, lifting me up, and getting me back on track when I'm filled with doubt. Love you!

To Steph, Cori, and Carolina. Thank you for letting this first-time author bounce contract questions off of you and for telling me "Do it!!!"

To my #TotallyFreeSVG Crew. You gals are amazing and you inspire me so much! The first Tuesday of the month is always a happy one for me thanks to all of you. Thanks for including me in your group and for inspiring me to push myself!

To my family, please make sure that you check out the dedication page, because this book is dedicated to you.

Thank you to my beautiful children, Bella and Adam, for being the most wonderful things that I ever created and for being my creative inspiration.

Thank you, Mom and Dad, for raising me in a creative home and for always supporting my dreams (no matter how crazy they were).

Thank you to my beautiful sister, Kara, for always being there for me and for our epic talks about life. Thank you also to her husband, Jimmy, for his generosity (and delicious farm produce) and to her two beautiful children, Jamie and Skye, for making me an aunt!

And finally thank you to my husband, Rob. You have been unwavering in your support and have never given me one reason to doubt that I should be doing exactly what I'm doing. You are the one and only reason that I am living my wildest dream to get to write and craft every day as a profession. Thank you. I love you.

About the Author

Crystal Allen is the owner and creative director of Hello Creative Family, a website for families looking to ignite their creativity with simple, playful, and fun crafts, DIYs, and recipes. Raised by two creative parents, Crystal is a firm believer that when kids see their parents pursuing their own creative passions, they are more likely to be creative themselves. It's that concept that is the driving force behind Hello Creative Family.

Crystal thinks that everyone has creativity within them, it's just about finding the right creative outlet for each person—whether that's in the kitchen, craft room, garden, workshop, or in the great outdoors.

With an emphasis on projects that take sixty minutes or less to make, Hello Creative Family's goal is to inspire families everywhere to carve out a bit of time to get creative and create a handmade, homemade, heart-made home.

A certified culinary nutrition expert with television training, Crystal teaches craft and cooking classes in her local community as well as sharing craft and food ideas on television. She is a lover of rainbow colors, sparkles, stickers, brightly colored Sharpies, books, dark chocolate, and tea.

Crystal resides in British Columbia, Canada, with her husband, Rob, her daughter, Bella, and son, Adam, and their rescue dog, Mochi.

Find more of Crystal and Hello Creative Family at:

Website: hellocreativefamily.com
Facebook: facebook.com/hellocreativefamily
Pinterest: pinterest.com/hellocreativef
Instagram: instagram.com/hellocreativefamily
By email: crystal@hellocreativefamily.com
Share your projects on instagram by tagging @hellocreativefamily and #caticorncrafts

TEMPLATES

We hope that you love these templates that we've created to help you create your caticorn crafts. Here are a few notes to help you use your templates effectively.

Tracing for Shrinky Dink projects: Place your shrink plastic directly on top of the designs that you would like to shrink, and trace the design onto your shrink plastic.

Tracing for paper crafts, fabric, or felt projects: Place a piece of tracing paper on top of the pattern piece that you want to use. Trace using a pencil. Use scissors to cut along your pencil marks so that you have a paper pattern piece. Lay your paper pattern piece on top of a piece of heavy card stock. Trace around the pattern piece using a pencil and then cut out using scissors. This will give you a heavy-duty template that you can use again and again. Trace around this template onto the material you are using for your caticorn project and then cut out.

Using a template to create a sticker: Use a scanner to scan the image you would like on your sticker. Print out onto sticker paper.

Find printable versions of all of these templates in various sizes at hellocreativefamily.com/caticorncrafts

General caticorn pieces

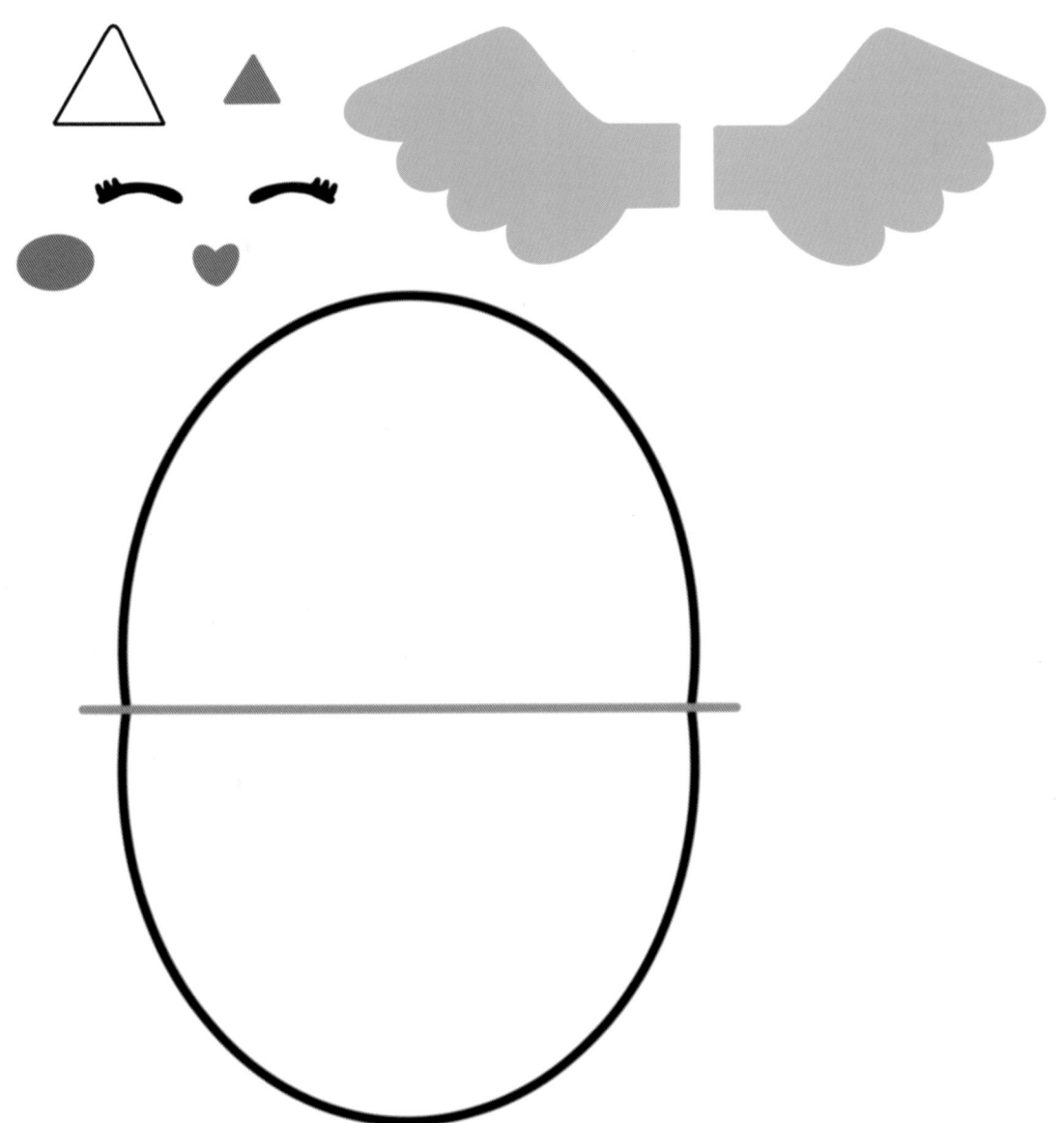

Sleepy Kitty No-Sew Sleep Mask, page 43. Use at size or print a large version at hellocreativefamily.com.

DIY Caticorn Letterboard Artwork,
page 69

You Are
Meow~gical

Strike a Purr-ty Pose Caticorn Masquerade Mask page 79. Use as sized or print a large version at hellocreativefamily.com.

Love the Purr-ty Planet Upcycled Caticorn Planter, page 91.

No-Sew Caticorn Cup Cozy, page 103.

Use me as inspiration for any of the projects in this book!

Use me as inspiration for any of the projects in this book!